Orde Wingate
And the British Internal Security Strategy
During the Arab Rebellion in Palestine,
1936-1939

A thesis presented to the Faculty of the U.S. Army
Command and General Staff College

by

MARK LEHENBAUER, MAJOR, US ARMY
B.S., Texas A&M University, College Station, Texas, 1999

Fort Leavenworth, Kansas
2012-01

The cover photo courtesy of the Library of Congress is that of General Dwight Eisenhower giving orders to American paratroopers in England.

Published by Books Express Publishing
Copyright © Books Express, 2012
ISBN 978-1-78266-063-7

Books Express publications are available from all good retail and online booksellers. For publishing proposals and direct ordering please contact us at: info@books-express.com

Abstract

Orde Wingate and the British Internal Security Strategy During the Arab Rebellion in Palestine, 1936-1939
By Major Mark Lehenbauer

The Arab Rebellion and British Counter-rebellion campaign of 1936 to 1939 in Palestine exhibited many features of modern insurgency and counterinsurgency. This thesis traces the British military thought and practice for countering rebellion as influenced by their Small Wars' experiences, and it then presents the rebellion and counter-rebellion campaign as a case study in their military and political contexts. This study focuses on the evolution of the internal security strategy, and it examines the actions of Captain Orde Wingate both within the campaign and in his attempts to influence it at the tactical, operational, and strategic levels. This research is intended to inform military practitioners about the campaign while highlighting the issues that are encountered when they seek to: (1) apply the contemporary wisdom of military thought and practice to a specific operational environment; (2) negotiate the policy constraints on the possible military "solutions" to the security problems incurred by insurgency; (3) influence various facets of the greater campaign when outside the hierarchy of responsibility and authority to do so; and (4) expose some of the issues involved with a counterinsurgent force's utilization of portions of the indigenous population toward converging interests. This study finds that Wingate sought to shape the evolving internal security strategy through both military and political channels, and that he utilized a variety of mechanisms to do so. Despite tactical successes in his validation of proofs of concept through the Special Night Squads, his determined efforts failed to achieve his stated goals at the operational and strategic levels.

Objectives of the Art of War Scholars Program

The Art of War Scholars Program is a laboratory for critical thinking. It offers a select group of students a range of accelerated, academically rigorous graduate level courses that promote analysis, stimulate the desire for life-long learning, and reinforce academic research skills. Art of War graduates will not be satisfied with facile arguments; they understand the complexities inherent in almost any endeavor and develop the tools and fortitude to confront such complexities, analyze challenges, and independently seek nuanced solutions in the face of those who would opt for cruder alternatives. Through the pursuit of these outcomes, the Art of War Scholars Program seeks to improve and deepen professional military education.

The Art of War Program places contemporary operations (such as those in Iraq and Afghanistan) in a historical framework by examining earlier military campaigns. Case studies and readings have been selected to show the consistent level of complexity posed by military campaigns throughout the modern era. Coursework emphasizes the importance of understanding previous engagements in order to formulate policy and doctrinal response to current and future campaigns.

One unintended consequence of military history education is the phenomenon of commanders and policy makers "cherry picking" history—that is, pointing to isolated examples from past campaigns to bolster a particular position in a debate, without a comprehensive understanding of the context in which such incidents occurred. This trend of oversimplification leaves many historians wary of introducing these topics into broader, more general discussion. The Art of War program seeks to avoid this pitfall by a thorough examination of context. As one former student stated: "The insights gained have left me with more questions than answers but have increased my ability to understand greater complexities of war rather than the rhetorical narrative that accompanies cursory study of any topic."

Professor Michael Howard, writing "The Use and Abuse of Military History" in 1961, proposed a framework for educating military officers in the art of war that remains unmatched in its clarity, simplicity, and totality. The Art of War program endeavors to model his plan:

Three general rules of study must therefore be borne in mind by the officer who studies military history as a guide to his profession and who wishes to avoid pitfalls. First, he must study in **width**. He must observe the way in which warfare has developed over a long historical period. Only by seeing what does change can one deduce what does not; and as much as can be learnt from the great discontinuities of military history as from the apparent similarities of the techniques employed by the great captains through the ages….Next he must study in **depth**. He should take a single campaign and explore it thoroughly, not simply from official histories, but from memoirs, letters, diaries. . . until the tidy outlines dissolve and he catches a glimpse of the confusion and horror of real experience... and, lastly, he must study in **context**. Campaigns and battles are not like games of chess or football matches, conducted in total detachment from their environment according to strictly defined rules. Wars are not tactical exercises writ large. They are...conflicts of societies, and they can be fully understood only if one understands the nature of the society fighting them. The roots of victory and defeat often have to be sought far from the battlefield, in political, social, and economic factors which explain why armies are constituted as they are, and why their leaders conduct them in the way they do....

It must not be forgotten that the true use of history, military or civil... is not to make men clever for the next time; it is to make them wise forever.

Gordon B. Davis, Jr.
Brigadier General, US Army
Deputy Commanding General
CAC LD&E

Daniel Marston
DPhil (Oxon) FRHistS
Ike Skelton Distinguished Chair
in the Art of War
US Army Command & General
Staff College

Acknowledgments

I owe a debt of appreciation to many for making this research both possible and a great experience. First and foremost, to my wife and children's support while daddy spent his time traveling, at the library, or "in the cave" researching, thinking and writing. The next cabal of individuals to whom I owe my appreciation are the military practitioners and student scholars who shared my experience in the Art of War Scholar's program at CGSC under the fearless leadership and incisive mentorship of our chair, Dr. Daniel Marston. This year not only proved to be one of a professional "renaissance" for me, but it has tremendously challenged and edified me as a professional. Dr. Stephenson and Dr. Murray from the Art of War cadre provided excellent (and much needed) constructive feedback.

I also owe a personal word of thanks to three exceptional men that greatly benefitted me by their generosity in time and patience to sit down and discuss my thoughts and questions while researching. I appreciate the scholarship and depth of research on Orde Wingate that has been conducted by Dr. Simon Anglim, the wisdom and insight of Dr. Matthew Hughes on the whole of my era of study, and the excellent conversation with Dr. Hew Strachan that leaves me at a loss to narrow down the many ways that he has influenced and contributed to my thought. Of course, despite the attributions, any and all errors or shortsightedness contained within this study are wholly mine.

Table of Contents

Abstract iii

Acknowledgments iv

Table of Contents vii

Glossary viii

Chapter 1 Introduction 1

Chapter 2: Military Thought and Practice for Countering
Rebellion in the British Army 7

Chapter 3: Operational Environment of Palestine
and the Grounds for Rebellion 23

Chapter 4: The Arab Rebellion
and Internal Security in Palestine 31

Chapter 5: Conclusions 83

Bibliography 93

Glossary

AO	Area of Operations
COIN	Counterinsurgency
GOC	General Officer Commanding
HC	High Commissioner
HM	His Majesty's
KIA	Killed in Action
SNS	Special Night Squads

Chapter 1
Introduction

> I first met Wingate when I took over command in Palestine in 1937 and found him on my Intelligence Staff. The name drew my attention at once, since I had known and admired his relation, General Sir Reginald Wingate. I enquired about him and was told he was rather an oddity, clever but eccentric; he had been in the Sudan for some years and knew Arabic well, but since coming to Palestine had developed pronounced Zionist tendencies and was now learning Yiddish or Hebrew. When I met him I realized that there was a remarkable personality behind those piercing eyes and rather abrupt manner. He was obviously no respecter of persons because of their rank. ... I left Palestine early in 1938, before he performed the exploits in defence of Jewish colonies which gained for him the D.S.O., but I carried away in a corner of my mind an impression of a notable character who might be valuable as a leader of unorthodox enterprise in war, if I should ever have need of one.[1]
> —Field Marshall Viscount Wavell, *Good Soldier*

The Arab Rebellion and British Counter-rebellion in Palestine from 1936 to 1939 provide many valuable features for a case study with issues of contemporary relevance. This study of the campaign and Orde Wingate's actions within it highlight the evolution of internal security strategy along with the ways in which that evolution can be influenced as it progresses. Because militaries often find themselves as the primary executors of nations' foreign policies in complex and challenging environments, the many facets of military practitioners' abilities to shape strategic approaches are of great significance. Lives, campaigns, and nations' interests rely on them. Some of these facets include the military officer's ability to (1) analyze the operational environment, (2) synthesize varied individual experiences with the collective experience of the military as an organization, and (3) apply both doctrine and the principles that have been distilled from the greater body of military knowledge as they pertain to their particular form of warfare and the campaign's context. These skills, in conjunction with the ability to both provide proofs of concept and to exercise influence, are assets of extreme relevance to military officers of all grades (and arguably more so in junior officers).

Wingate's analysis of the operational environment led to his own development of tactical methods and operational concepts. His assessment of the overarching strategic goals for Palestine within the British Empire put him at odds with the official assessment and goals pursued. At every level, Wingate sought to influence the greater campaign. His actions in Palestine highlight the issues concerning the way in which strategy can be influenced by those outside the hierarchy of responsibilities and authorities to do so, or from the bottom up. His actions in London highlight the challenges, risks, and issues of propriety associated with an officer of his rank and position interjecting assessments straight to the "top."

The Arab Rebellion

The Arab Rebellion and British Counter-rebellion Campaign themselves are a particularly valuable case study with contemporary relevance for three reasons. First, the rebellion was composed of many of the complexities that mark some of the most difficult aspects of insurgencies in modern times. These included:

1. Political organization that was used to foment and instigate violence against the governing power;

2. The population's ethnic and religious composition along sectarian lines;

3. The population's varied political composition that led to numerous and competing political organizations with both the potential and practice of alliances and fractures;

4. The rebel militants' employment of guerrilla tactics, sabotage of infrastructure, captured weapons, and improvised explosive devices;

5. The presence of a clandestine insurgent infrastructure able to sustain a campaign of violence; and

6. Insurgent sanctuary and support afforded by foreign countries.

Second, the composition of the military forces available to implement an internal security strategy were sufficiently modern enough to deal with many of the doctrinal, organizational, and operational challenges that endure until today. The composition of forces and the ways in which they employed force were paramount to formulating military solutions for the identified security problems. Third, political considerations led to an increased need for civil-military cooperation in applying synergistic political and military solutions, but these sensitivities also led to a civil-military relationship that was often tenuous. Deliberations between the military and civil authorities over policy and security actions were constantly requiring the exertion of attention and energy both within and between governmental bodies. In typical British practice up to this point, the authorities and responsibilities for decisions on both security and political matters were both to be found in the hands of either the military command or the civil government. The other party would act only in an advisory role. During the Arab Rebellion, however, the emergence of new practices for delineating these responsibilities line by line would create administrative lag-times, loopholes, and power struggles between the military and other governmental bodies. Regardless of the overarching decision-making relationships, the impact of policy restrictions on the available military options for resolving security issues generated friction within the military. These restrictions also raised questions as to the appropriateness of methods and channels or challenging policy for change.

There are a few well-researched works on the Arab Rebellion that are set in the contexts of Arab and Jewish politics, the Arab national movement in Palestine, and the evolution of Zionist politics toward their realization of statehood. Respectively, these primary works have been written by J.C. Hurewitz, Yehoshua Porath, and Christopher Sykes. Tom Bowden has added two key works for understanding the security apparatus in Palestine during this period, one with a focus on the maintenance of public security against organized political violence and another with regard to the state of the Palestine Police prior to 1936. Less is known about the inner workings of the Arab Rebellion itself, though Hurewitz and Porath draw from many of the available primary sources in Arabic to reconstruct what can be known. The British and Jewish perspectives are well documented from primary source material and memoirs. In this case study, as it focuses on the evolution and implementation of the internal security strategy, primary sources are heavily relied upon from both the official British documents along with correspondence and documents produced by the military and governmental officials that influenced it.

Orde Wingate

Orde Wingate was a relatively junior officer in Palestine and never held a position of official capacity within which he shared the military responsibilities and authorities for contributing to the internal security strategy. This point, however, is particularly what makes his actions there of interest and relevance to many modern military practitioners. Consistently throughout his career, Wingate was a controversial figure. This is often attributed to his relative unorthodoxy in relation to more conventional military approaches. The fundamental elements of his military thought and practice, however, do not appear to greatly depart from the contemporary military thought as influenced by British military tradition.[2] The individual experiences and personalities of able commanders are often catalysts to clashes of opinion on the "proper" strategy to be employed and the emphasis that they emplace upon its ends, ways, and means. While they often seek to shore up their arguments on grounds of historical soundness and current practicalities, they are often more wed to their ideas and opinions because of intangibles. These include what they interpret as being "learned" from experience, their own operational style, their own ideological and/or political beliefs, and differences in their understanding of the operational environment whether subtle or blatant. While none of these intangibles can be argued as absolutes, they prove to be pivotal influences on how a military officer interprets what "right looks like."

Wingate's eccentric personality has also added to his controversial legacy both among those who knew him and until today. His rather odd propensities and pointed communication style have resulted in many an apologia from those praising him for exhibiting military genius. Others have been less nuanced in distinguishing the whole of the man from his military actions, noting little if any distinction in their condemnation for what they considered as maniacal tendencies through and through. Notable among Wingate's military critics was the Field Marshall William Slim, while many military friends and subordinates have written in his defense to include the counterinsurgency (COIN) expert Sir Robert Thompson who worked with Wingate's unit in Burma.

Wingate is most widely recognized for his actions during World War II in Burma where he died commanding nearly 20,000 soldiers behind Japanese lines as a Major General. This pinnacle event in conjunction with the controversies that he always seemed to leave in his wake has resulted in two overarching approaches to Wingate's historiography. The first has been to view the whole of his military career through the lens of his actions in Burma. This approach has produced many of the works most pertinent to the military historian and practitioner, but it has also led to a mere highlighting of previous events that were deemed relevant to understanding his later actions as the Chindit Commander. A second approach is also typical among his biographers. Though many of the details of his life and career prior to Burma have been well researched in these works, they often over-emphasize the leitmotif of Wingate's personality necessitating that he always act as the contrarian and maverick. The most useful of these biographies to the military historian and practitioner are the ones by Trevor Royle and Christopher Sykes because of the depth and breadth of their research. The historian and author Simon Anglim should be noted as of special interest to the military historian and practitioner for his significant contribution to the body of research and thought on Wingate both during and prior to Burma. This is not only because of the research found within his numerous works on Wingate, but because of the analysis.

Methodology and Thesis

This study will treat the entirety of the Arab Rebellion and British Counter-rebellion Campaign in Palestine from 1936 to 1939 as a case study because it relies on an explanation of the relevant military and political contexts for understanding the internal security strategy that was employed. This approach, therefore, will first cover topical issues of relevance that influenced the British Military thought and practice of its day before presenting a chronological account of the rebellion and counter-rebellion campaign. Within this framework, Wingate's actions will be woven into the evolution and implementation of the internal security strategy as it unfolded to include consideration of both the significance of his attempts to influence the strategy along with the means and channels he used. The goals for this research are to provide a case study sufficient to inform military practitioners about this campaign while highlighting the seemingly timeless issues that are encountered when a practitioner seeks to:

1. Apply the contemporary wisdom of military thought and practice to a specific operational environment without necessarily being bound within the proverbial "box";

2. Negotiate the policy constraints on the possible military "solutions" to the security problems incurred by insurgency; and

3. Expose the issues of a military force in using portions of the indigenous population towards converging interests.

This study finds that Wingate sought to shape the evolving internal security strategy through both military and political channels. Wingate's bottom-up approach conducted through military channels was two-tiered. Through a successful series of proofs-of-concept, Wingate validated the employment of unique organization and methods capable of tactically interdicting and defeating rebel bands upon contact. This was accomplished through Wingate's emphasis on employing small-unit, nighttime patrolling, and assault techniques from tactical formations composed of British Soldiers and Jewish supernumerary police. Wingate's operational plan for widespread neutralization of the rebel bands with the goal of bringing rural areas under governmental control was never realized through his intentions for the expansion of the organization and dissemination of the tactics employed. Failing in this, Wingate sought to influence the overarching strategy and policy with which he was at odds and that he had determined to be the limiting factor. Wingate engaged the military and political policy-makers as well as those that were influential among them in a top-down attempt to accomplish this. Wingate's failed attempts to impact the internal security strategy in Palestine were a result of:

1. The failure of widespread adoption of his tactics due to a surge in British Military Forces which rendered the tactical risks inherent in his methods to be deemed unacceptable;

2. The prevention of his organization's operational expansion due to a policy that restricted both the strength and types of employment of Jews within the security forces; and

3. The loss of trust from the military command toward Wingate due to his crossing the accepted boundary of a military official's obligation to submit his own opinions to established policy.

Notes

1. Archibald Wavell, *Good Soldier* (London: MacMillan, 1948), 62. Wavell would later need just such a character and leader, and not only once but twice. He would call upon Wingate for action in Ethiopia and again in Burma.

2. Simon Anglim, *Orde Wingate and the British Army, 1922-1944* (London: Pickering & Chatto, 2010), 17-18. Anglim's driving research question was "how far did the military thought and practice and Major General OC Wingate really part company with British Army doctrine of his time?" His short answer was "not as much as some people claim" as he sought to "establish Wingate's true 'place' in British military tradition."

Chapter 2
Military Thought and Practice for Countering Rebellion in the British Army

"Big Wars" and "Small Wars"

The orientation of the British Army leading up to the Arab Rebellion in Palestine between 1936 and 1939 was a result of long-standing threats both to the homeland and to its interests and territories throughout the empire. The need to maintain and re-prioritize various capabilities led to organizational and managerial reforms that were enacted before World War I.[1] One such reform created the regimental system in order to allow units to be employed on a rotating basis between home and overseas assignments, where up to half of the army was required to garrison the empire at any given time.[2] While it was necessary for the army to be an expeditionary force to counter threats both on the European Continent and within the greater empire, few other similarities existed between the challenges that were posed in preparing for and waging either "big wars" or "small wars." The *Field Service Regulations* of 1930 state "the British Empire is confronted with problems peculiarly its own. Unlike a continental power, it consists mainly of a number of self-governing communities widely separated and of varying resources. In defence of its vital interests it may be called upon to place a force in the field under conditions varying from a small expedition against an uncivilized enemy to a world-wide war."[3]

Big Wars were classified as major land wars against first-rate opponents that were organized along relatively symmetrical bases. Small Wars, on the other hand, included various types of expeditions and security missions against external and internal threats to territories abroad that harbored British interests.[4] Initially, the primary distinction was that Small Wars would consist of military forces employed against "irregular, or comparatively speaking irregular, forces."[5] There was no differentiation between the degrees of force to be applied in war whether Big or Small. Small Wars entailed the use of the military to undertake "deliberate campaigns with a definite military objective ... [with] no limitations .... placed on the amount of force which [could] legitimately be exercised. ..."[6]

Subsets of the Small Wars tradition would progressively be introduced that challenged these initial and primary bases for distinction. These subsets were delineated for two primary reasons. First, different and unique sets of tactics were required for the variations encountered in terms of the terrain and enemy. Second, the presence of an acting British Civil Government over the territory in which the military action was to be conducted introduced a peculiarly new set of requirements. This type of political environment necessitated both cooperation and delineation of authorities between the military and civil instruments of British power. The degree to which such civil governments required military assistance was a primary determinant for both the framework in which the cooperation would take place and how the authorities would be distributed. These issues constituted a primary concern for Britain when countering rebellion during the interwar period. They would also determine which governmental entities would drive the internal security strategy as well as the authorities that they had in implementing it. They are thus a primary concern for this thesis. Two Small Wars subsets of particular importance came to be defined by the terms of military operations conducted in support of an acting civil government. These were "imperial policing" and "acting in the aid to the civil power." These types of military operations were conducted as part of an internal security strategy that was determined by the civil government under the advisement of the military for dealing with security issues. When the acting civil government was no longer viable due to extreme deterioration of the security situation, the military could then be granted the full authority and responsibility for both governing and restoring order until the civil government could be restored.

The Evolution of Small Wars Doctrine and the Doctrinal Gap

Until as recently as 1989, none of the British army's longstanding and unique bodies of experience and knowledge found themselves to be truly codified into comprehensive written doctrine, at least not in terms of how it was coming to be accepted among Western nations.[7] The *Field Service Regulations* of 1909 was the first such debut of official British Doctrine, but it negotiated the varied needs of British Military Officers by taking a deliberately nonprescriptive approach. General principles were set forth for the conduct of war, but the emphasis was on the commander's use of his experience and judgment for application. Despite the fact that Small Wars were the predominant British Army experience throughout this period, only one chapter was devoted to them in the *Field Service Regulations*. Publications specific to the imperial experience and even to particular campaigns would later come into being in order to address the peculiarities of Small Wars and their multiple subsets. These publications filled some of the void for guidance on Small Wars, but there were identifiable gaps between the ever-expanding experiences and the official publications.[8] These official publications specific to Small Wars subsets were eventually embodied in rather short works such as *Duties in Aid to the Civil Power* (1923 and 1937), *Notes on Imperial Policing* (1934), and *Operations on the North-West Frontier* (1925).[9]

It should not be assumed, however, that a lack of official doctrine was widely acknowledged as a problem during this era. There even appears to have been resistance to such doctrine caused by practical obstacles such as the organization of the force. The regimental idiosyncrasies created an environment that elevated a subunit's collective experience and tradition.

This aspect of British Military culture flouted even worthy attempts to systematize a common operating doctrine.[10] A few key influential writings appeared before the official publications that captured the greater British Small Wars experience. They would significantly contribute not only to the development of the doctrinal publications but to the military thought and practice in countering the Arab Rebellion of 1936 to 1939. The counter-rebellion campaign would even produce its own semidoctrinal publications covering not only the organizational and tactical lessons learned, but histories of the political events and assessments that shaped the conflict.

There is much agreement among historians concerning the fact that the British Army was guided in its conduct of war more by "pragmatism and expedience, not [by] theory" or prescriptive doctrine.[11] Alternate and unofficial bodies of wisdom, however, existed to help guide officers in the employment of their organization and the force that they could bring to bear. These publications consisted of historical case studies, collations of "best practice" methods, unofficial "doctrine," professional journals, and the writings by theorists such as B. H. Liddell Hart and J. F. C. Fuller.[12] The key works among the Small Wars literature that acted as unofficial doctrine were first and foremost those written by Colonel C. E. Calwell and Major General Sir Charles Gwynn. Lieutenant Colonel H. J. Simson would continue the Small Wars literature tradition in a work contemporaneous with the Arab Rebellion.

Calwell's *Small Wars: Their Principles and Practice* was published in three editions between 1896 and 1906, and it was long held as the most definitive work on the subject. Calwell chose to communicate his extensive Small Wars experience and study through 559 pages full of historical references that provide the basis for his conclusions.[13] Gwynn's *Imperial Policing* was published in 1934 and includes two short chapters titled "The Nature of the Army's Police Duties" and "Principles and Doctrine" which are then followed by 10 chapters of case studies.[14] Simson would later write *British Rule, and Rebellion* in 1937, whereby he introduced the concept of "sub-war" and explored the types and logic of available political and military responses to this emerging form of warfare, followed by a critical case study of the British response to the Arab Revolt in 1936.[15] These works, in conjunction with the official publications, comprised the most complete bodies of thought of this period dealing with conflict short of a Big War. It will be necessary to address these works in further detail, but first the methodological approach to Small Wars literature both requires an explanation and offers an insight into how they aided the practitioner in application of their works.

A significant contribution of Small Wars literature appears to be in the approach that it took toward preparing and equipping the army to best utilize the aspects of their tradition, experiences, and best practices that were earned over a long history of conducting Small Wars. The means of communication included a combination of emphasis and style in translating the depth and detail of Small Wars history into conclusions offered as summarized concepts. In general, two historically based methodologies were used. The first was of brief and broad principles that were either accompanied by long lists of case studies selected for their relevance by virtue of the types of operations conducted and/or their regional focus. The second was one of pithy points that captured first-hand experiences or lessons digested from study, and these were then accompanied by the historical references that provided the basis for their detailed examination, explanations, and conclusions on the subject. This literature was intended to provide a vicarious experience in addition to that of the reader's experience in order to inform the proper judgment and to be used according to the particular circumstances for application. This practice is evidenced through publications chronicling both specific campaigns and ongoing security challenges throughout the empire. The *Notes on the Tactical Lessons of the Palestine Rebellion, 1936* states that "The tactics based on North-West Frontier principles, with common sense modifications, to suit local conditions, are the most suitable."[16]

The use of unofficial doctrine and the multiple adjuncts that were eventually made to compliment the *Field Service Regulations* in addressing subsets of Small Wars highlights that there are inherent difficulties in codifying a useable and widely applicable Small Wars Doctrine. Callwell acknowledges the universality of ideas such as "principles of war" that were derived from studying war in general, but he goes on to specifically note that "the conditions of small wars are so diversified, the enemy's mode of fighting is often so peculiar, and the theaters of operations present such singular features, that irregular warfare must generally be carried out on a method totally different," and that the "conduct of small wars is in fact in certain respects an art by itself. ... " He adds that "the strategical problems presented by operations of this nature have not altered to [a great] extent. Therefore there is much belonging to this branch of the military art still to be learnt from campaigns dating as far back as the conquest of Algeria and as the terrible Indian struggle of 1857-58. ..." He concludes that principles "can be learnt from the military history of early times just as well as it can be learnt from the more voluminously chronicled struggles of the present epoch."[17]

Based on the track record of successful British Small Wars campaigns that were guided with the aid of Small Wars literature, modern practitioners of warfare that are Small Wars legacies might consider the significance of this historically based approach. Equipping military officers in depth and width of relevant military history accomplishes two important functions. It enhances both their judgment in application of their doctrine and their ability to apply critical evaluation of the transferability of historical "lessons" from one context to another.[18]

Countering Rebellion: Enduring Concepts as a Legacy of Small Wars

Countering rebellion composed a great deal of Britain's Small Wars experiences. Significant aspects of this experience have been translated into the modern body of knowledge known as counterinsurgency, or COIN. Thomas Mockaitis, a historian with extensive research on the legacy of British Small Wars and the development of COIN methods and principles both before and during the classic COIN theorists of the mid-20th century, identifies the imperial era's three most pertinent contributions to modern COIN wisdom.[19] He summarizes these concepts as "minimum force, civil-military cooperation and tactical flexibility."[20] Each of these concepts requires further explanation to clarify both how they were understood and how they influenced the thought and practice of countering rebellion during the inter-war period. Such a discussion is incomplete and inadequate for the practitioner, however, without an emphasis on context and application.

Internal Security Strategy: Concepts in Context and Application

The concepts of "minimum force," "civil-military cooperation," and "tactical flexibility" each have long histories that predate the Arab Rebellion. They have evolved and continue to evolve over time. As they do so, they have necessarily been contemporized but not always beneficially summarized as buzzwords and simple phrases. The value in these concepts, however, is not easily translated into contemporary wisdom apart from understanding the contexts in which they were wrought. These contexts highlight the continuities and changes that have taken place within the concepts themselves, as well as the frictions that are inherent in the details of applying them. The contexts bring the concepts to life as the challenges of their application are shown to be inseparable from the practitioners' interaction with the specific dynamics of a campaign.

The military practitioner's understanding of his contemporary operational environment is the first imperative in the application of historically derived military concepts and principles. From this proceeds his identification of the "military" problem for which a solution can be brought to bear, though it must be borne in mind that the social, political, economic, and military situations in countering rebellion tend to be inextricably linked. The process of applying conceptual principles in war, which is dialectic, plays itself out in strategy. For countering rebellion, this strategy is inherently concerned with internal security. Strategy includes the employment of the organization and the force that it can bring to bear in its tactical methods and operational goals toward achievement of the desired strategic end-state.[21] Changes in the variables throughout this process over time require constant reassessment and readjustment to the overall internal security strategy if it is to achieve and maintain coherence and synergy. It is important to bear in mind that the levels of war which strategy must address in its component parts are not strictly hierarchic in terms of importance, nor is the process of the formulation of strategy strictly chronological.[22] Furthermore, the formulation of strategy is often not purely a military endeavor because it is not strictly concerned with only military and security matters. Because this is often the case, the military has a duty to advise the policy-makers on the effects of their policy as it interacts with each of the levels of war. Sometimes policies are determined by the military as detrimental to military goals. When the military's assessment of the political considerations that shaped those policies are at odds with the policy-makers, then the military has a duty to attempt to influence a change of policy. When the military has failed to achieve this or is awaiting policy change, they must negotiate the effects of policy directives and limitations on the available solutions to the military problem.

Minimum Force

During the Arab Rebellion, the concept of "minimum force" had been well established in the literature and publications most recently and thoroughly up to that point by Gwynn.[23] Minimum force was relative to what was deemed to be required to successfully achieve the desired effects. It was primarily concerned with the military's application of force as it related to the legal authorities for employing it. It should also be borne in mind that the concept's impact on the military thought took place in an era of relatively less prohibitions than today.[24] The general framework of opinion was that aggressive action was required early in the response to internal threats to security and stability.[25] While actions needed to be taken within the legal framework, this rested on a legal repertoire of potential military authorities and powers that allowed for strict (even draconian) laws to be emplaced. The implications were that force and judicial punishments could be employed generously, if necessary, toward the achievement of their desired effects.[26] The *Manual of Military Law*, 1929, states "The existence of an armed insurrection would justify the use of any degree of force necessary effectually to meet and cope with the insurrection."[27]

The cautionary tone of minimum force is derived from the fact that military actions in countering rebellion have political, social, and economic impacts that directly correlate to the achievement of the desired strategic end-state. The experiences of the interwar period would be added to later experiences leading to a general acceptance of caution in modern COIN against an overly militarized approach towards the problems of counter-rebellion. This was not yet fully apparent in the interwar period. The military thought of the time was encountering the emergence of new kinds of real and perceived political realities. This resulted in tensions that were growing between the military and other governmental bodies who played significant roles in policy-making. The former often wanted to use traditional military methods and available legal authorities in suppressing rebellion, whereas the latter wanted to tighten their control over military actions to mitigate anticipated political fallout. This control was exercised through policies that directed or restricted the particular types of security operations to be conducted, the organization of the forces employed, and the employment of force itself.[28]

Gwynn takes particular note of junior officers when addressing the issue of minimum force. He notes that "Responsibility is often thrown on quite junior officers for the action necessary. Mistakes of judgment may have far-reaching consequences."[29] Gwynn endeavors to define the differences between what is required of officers in Imperial Policing versus traditional military operations. Beyond his observation of the fact that they "must rely on their own judgment to reconcile military action with the political conditions," he states that "as a rule, they have to decide what is the minimum force they must employ rather than how they can develop the maximum power at their disposal."[30]

Such caution was (and still is) prescient while countering rebellion (and conducting COIN campaigns) due to the roles that intangibles play. Attention to important concepts such as public opinion and legitimacy of the government in the eyes of the population have long been prevalent and respected for their role in achieving success in the counter-rebellion "fight."[31] Such considerations were clearly linked to the long-term political objectives of restoring peace and stability among a pacified population. The practical military benefits were likewise argued against those with a predilection for the use of overwhelming force to solve most security situations.[32] Intelligence for operations is derived from a cooperative portion of the population, and this is potentially jeopardized through excessive severity in the application of military force. Further, the military's use of indiscriminate or imprecise application of force could result in a boon to insurgent recruiting.[33] The rebels' use of the media and propaganda in exploiting real, perceived, or contrived uses of excessive force was yet another contributing factor for the caution.[34]

In conjunction with these practical military concerns, the era of the Arab Rebellion in Palestine was witnessing an enlarged stage upon which war in general was being played out. "Political" concerns have always been present in war with varying degrees of direct impact on the ends, ways, and means for and by which wars are to be conducted. The notion that binds politics and war is most clearly defined as the use of military force as an element of national power to further policy aims, and pointed out by Carl von Clausewitz as an essential part of the very nature of war itself.[35] The recognition of particular political influences on the campaign in Palestine was captured in an official military publication titled the *Military Lessons of the Arab Rebellion in Palestine, 1936*. A chapter on

"Conditions in Palestine as Affecting Operations" specifically highlights the powerful influences upon the campaign resulting from heightened international attention among both the Western and the Arab worlds, the intertwined racial and religious facets of the internal politics there, and the enormous impact of propaganda and the media.[36] The difficulties presented by these factors were beginning to take on a magnitude of importance that is better understood today in light of COIN experience, but at the time it was just beginning to reveal a collision between traditional Small Wars practices and increasing policy limitations placed upon commanders.

The policy limitations resulting from these political sensitivities that were in conflict with traditional military applications of force created a paradox for a commander. Guerrillas needed to be "hunted down," and measures needed to be taken to separate them from the population.[37] There was also the argument that "Anything which can be interpreted as weakness encourages those who are sitting on the fence to keep on good terms with the rebels."[38] Political agitators and persons providing support to the rebels, though nonviolent in and of themselves, were much more difficult to handle both militarily and legally. Inaction would allow the rebel infrastructure to remain intact, while strong action would invariably lead to negative consequences for innocents among the population. The resulting problem of counter-rebellion campaigns, where there is tension between the necessity of both restraint and aggression, is not one that modern COIN theory has mastered though the vocabulary, arguments and logic have become more nuanced. For the purposes of this study, it is sufficient to point out that today there is a perceptible distinction in both the terms and their associated frameworks for applying force in (1) COIN operations as a whole on the one hand, and (2) counterguerrilla (sometimes described as counterterrorist or countergang) operations which can either be a subset or conducted entirely outside of COIN on the other. Counterguerrilla operations have taken on an appreciation in modern times of precision targeting and isolated concentrations of force against militant guerrillas.

Civil-Military Cooperation

An understanding of "civil-military cooperation," again in its proper context, must also take into account the available arrangements for authorities and responsibilities over the handling of internal security crises. While the policy of the government was to be carried out regardless of the framework for the division of duties and powers between civil and military authorities, the military's role was acknowledged to be a significant one toward the formulation and execution of internal security policies. The spectrum of military obligations and authorities were primarily dependent upon:

1. Whether existing civil laws were in effect under a functioning government over a relatively pacified population; or

2. Martial law had been instated due to a breakdown in public security and loss of civil control.

The former would entail the military's responsibility to render advice to the civil administration concerning the effects of policy on security considerations, while the latter entailed full military authorities over both security issues and the civil administration.[39] Variations between the extremes in the scope of authorities granted to the civil government and the military during the Arab Rebellion in Palestine would be described as resembling "a rainbow, [with] the shades of colour merging so gently that it is hard to say where one ends and the next begins."[40]

Gwynn not only highlights civil-military cooperation as one of the four major principles to guide the successful conduct of Imperial Policing, but he notes that the "duty of giving advice [to the government] may often fall on quite junior [military] officers."[41] Though the immediate context of this statement is that the advice rendered would be from a junior military officer to the civil authorities, the statement can be assumed to be dependent upon the size of the military force employed and the command hierarchies in place. It can be inferred that this same advice could be beneficial within the military ranks as well, regardless of strength and structure. Whether in yesterday's counter-rebellion or today's COIN campaigns, matters of policy and strategy are closely intertwined with tactical considerations involving the composition of forces and the employment of force. Junior officers are the ones in contact with both the rebels (insurgents) and the population as well. Collectively, junior officers hold the knowledge of the "ground truth" that in turn may or may not be sufficiently communicated up the levels of command, where a comprehensive picture of the operational environment should reside. Junior officers' experiences of policy limitations on the military objectives that they're literally living and dying to achieve, show no distinction between the cliché and reality of "fighting with one hand tied behind their back." It is not a stretch to assume that they were, on the whole, not always privy to the deliberations that resulted in these decisions. Rules of engagement, requirements and/ or prohibitions to work with indigenous forces, and "no-hit" lists are just a few of the arenas where the junior officer and soldier meet policy on a day-to-day basis.

Tactical Flexibility

Mockaitis states that the collective wisdom of the British Army during this period demonstrated that "Warfare against elusive insurgents requires small-unit operations, tactical flexibility and a high caliber of junior leadership. ..."[42] These characteristics are less in need of explanatory caveats that were due to the peculiarities of the period than the aforementioned modern COIN principles that were derived from the Small Wars experience. An enduring element in campaigns of countering rebellion is that junior leaders leading small units are at the point of friction between the rebels and those countering rebellion. Guerrilla operations short of a "war of movement" often employ small-unit organization in order to elude and evade larger military formations, which inevitably leads to decentralized and small-unit actions to take their place among military "best practices." This is a particularly relevant point to the counterguerrilla operations that are necessary as an element of a campaign to counter rebellion. Irregular enemies and unconventional tactics often require a departure from yesterday's Big Wars and today's "conventional" approaches in both the organization and tactics employed. The requirements for such operations have taken on an appreciation in modern times that has led to the use of Special Operations Forces that combine such features as select individuals for the force, habitual work with indigenous personnel, and specialized organization, training, equipment, modes of employment and operational techniques. The distinctions during the Arab Rebellion were present in the tradition of assembling ad hoc units for specific operations, though they had not yet developed into the practice of standing up enduring organizations with focused mission-sets as seen in more modern times.

Present during the British response to the Arab Rebellion was the legacy of employing a specially trained unit formed around "the man" to overcome tactical problems that were not readily answered within the capabilities and limitations of the security forces paradigm. Security forces normally consisted of the separate organizations of military, police, and auxiliary security forces (the latter two often being composed in part or whole of indigenous personnel). This paradigm, if strictly adhered to in practice, resulted in a blurring of the lines of the "police" and "military" duties. Tactical dilemmas would often be a catalyst for the British to improvise the right organization with the right capabilities to leverage force in countering rebellion. Charles Townshend comments that the "deleterious effect of militarizing the police on the one hand, and of using soldiers as policemen on the other, naturally raised the question of creating a 'third force' which would be neither one nor the other. The obvious attractions of such a hybrid force, matching the hybrid legal state of 'emergency,' produced repeated discussions and experiments."[43] In Mockaitis' words, Britain "has a history of creating hybrid forces to recoup deteriorating situations. ... "[44]

Application of Doctrine and Learned Principles in Countering Rebellion

After posing the question "How are officers to be trained for such [Imperial Policing] duties?", Gwynn continues, "It is hardly possible to draw up exercises in which the work can be practiced. One can formulate general principles, but the difficulty lies in providing opportunities of learning to apply them." He further states, "In the absence of literature on the subject, tradition becomes the only means of broadcasting experience, and tradition is apt to be based on experience limited to a small number of cases ... [and] it has its dangers."[45] Gwynn's statements identify the inherent difficulties and complexities of countering rebellion and he inquires on the means by which an officer can be prepared for conducting it.

To continue along his line of thinking, a few additional points are worth noting. The first is that more "literature" does not necessarily mean that the experience it captures is any better than one's tradition, though it should increase the chances of finding relevant lessons learned. Experience is helpful, whether personal or learned from others, but the "right" experience is particularly key. Principles are helpful, but they are only as useful as they can be applied effectively to the situation at hand. It is "dangerous" to assume one's own experience is superior to that of others or what might be found in the literature. It is also dangerous to assume that effective application of the principles can take place apart from a deep appreciation of the particularities of the operational environment at hand. It can be assumed, therefore, that countering rebellion will often require a campaign commander to not only be willing to look outside of his own experiences and understanding but to probe the environment, assume risk, experiment, and underwrite the mistakes of others in the search for success.

The legacy of the Small Wars experience, with its most pertinent points up to the Arab Rebellion being captured by the literature, highlights the long-standing recognition of the inherent difficulties in countering rebellion. The significance of considerations concerning minimum force, civil-military cooperation, and tactical flexibility were understood to be crucial elements of a campaign to counter rebellion during the Arab Rebellion. These Small Wars contributions to COIN doctrine, which continue to gain wide acceptance through nearly a century of experience, emphasize the fact that even the combination of identified issues and time-tested guidance are still difficult to apply towards a military solution.

In countering rebellion, military officers will be required to:

1. Effectively employ force to achieve its desired effects with minimal negative repercussions;

2. Inform and influence policy-makers with regard to the policies and their effects on the campaign; and

3. Understand and exploit the tactical strengths and weaknesses between one's own force and that of the enemy.

These actions rely upon a military practitioner's thorough understanding of the operational environment. The practitioner benefits from an in-depth understanding of the hard-won principles that are available to guide his judgment in their application. The classic COIN theorist Frank Kitson summarizes the gravity of these points by commenting that "Military commanders in counter-insurgency operations cannot do without a real understanding of this sort of war in the widest sense."[46] He further adds, "There is no single thing more important than being able to size up the situation, as it exists, and make the best of it." The operational environment in Palestine between 1936 and 1939 would challenge many officers that would later prove their skill and proficiency as able commanders in World War II and include Montgomery, O'Connor, Dill, and Wavell. The Arab Rebellion would present a magnitude of challenges not only peculiarly its own, but of a more general type that the British had only first begun to encounter in Northern Ireland in 1920 to 1921 and would later routinely experience as those associated with the modern complexities inherent in COIN.

Notes

1. Hew Strachan, "The British Way in Warfare," *Oxford History of the British Army* (Oxford: Oxford University Press, 1994), 403-408; David French, "Big wars and small wars between the wars, 1919-39," in *Big Wars and Small Wars: The British army and the lessons of war in the twentieth century*, ed. Hew Strachan (London: Routledge, 2006), 38.

2. Philip J. Haythornthwaite, *The Colonial Wars Source Book* (London: Arms and Armour, 2007), 17-20.

3. War Office, *Field Service Regulations*. Vol. 1. (Organization and Administration) (London: War Office, 1930), 1-2 as cited in David French, "Big wars and small wars between the wars, 1919-39," in *Big Wars and Small Wars: The British army and the lessons of war in the twentieth century,* ed. Hew Strachan, (London: Routledge, 2006), 36.

4. *Training Regulations* (London: War Office, 1934), 1; Major General Sir Charles Gwynn, *Imperial Policing* (London: Macmillan and Co., 1935), 3-4. While incipient definitions of modern terms that recognize categories and sub-categories of war and tactics have long been present, these can be confused with modern developments and interpretations of the terms. This study will use the terms of the period at hand. Definitions will be offered as either those defined or widely accepted at the time, or those clarified through the distinctions made by the primary sources consulted for this study. To apply modern definitions to some of the types of warfare encountered and the operations conducted in "small wars" which included countering rebellion, one would find irregular warfare in terms of both the use of indigenous forces and the varieties of enemy combatants, as well as counter-insurgency, counter-guerrilla and counter-terrorism operations among others.

5. C. E. Callwell, *Small Wars: Their Principles and Practice* (London: Harrison and Sons, 1906), 21

6. Charles Gwynn, *Imperial Policing,* 3.

7. For an overview of the British doctrinal approach and evolution over the period concerned, see Alex Alderson, "The Validity of British Army Counterinsurgency Doctrine after the War in Iraq 2003-2009" (Ph.D dissertation, Cranfield University, 2009), 35-41, 99-103; Hew Strachan, "The British Way in Warfare," *Oxford History of the British Army* (Oxford: Oxford University Press, 1994), 404-405, 411; David French, "Big wars and small wars between the wars, 1919-39," in *Big Wars and Small Wars: The British Army and the Lessons of War in the Twentieth Century,* Hew Strachan, editor (London: Routledge, 2006), 36-41.

8. David French, "Big wars and small wars between the wars, 1919-39," 40-41; Alderson, "The Validity of British Army Counterinsurgency Doctrine after the War in Iraq 2003-2009," 38-39, 99-103.

9. These documents are referenced within the internal War Office publications specific to the Palestine campaign such as *Notes on Tactical Lessons of the Palestine Rebellion, 1936,* and *Military Lesson of the Arab Rebellion in Palestine, 1936.*

10. French "Big wars and small wars between the wars, 1919-39," 42.

11. Strachan, "The British Way in Warfare," 400; French, "Big wars and small wars between the wars, 1919-39," 40.

12. Anglim, *Orde Wingate and the British Army, 1922-1944*, 23. Anglim's Chapter 2, "The Doctrinal Background," provides an excellent survey of British army doctrine while the book as a whole addresses the question as to whether Wingate's military thought and practice was a departure from it (see 17).

13. See Callwell, *Small Wars: Their Principles and Practice*.

14. See Gwynn, *Imperial Policing*.

15. H. J. Simson, *British Rule and Rebellion* (Edinburgh: William Blackwood & Sons Ltd., 1937).

16. *Notes on Tactical Lessons of the Palestine Rebellion, 1936* (War Office, February 1937), 8.

17. Callwell, *Small Wars: Their Principles and Practice*, 23.

18. See Michael Howard, "The Use and Abuse of Military History," *RUSI Journal* (February 1993, reprint from 1961): 29-30.

19. Classic COIN theorists widely accepted for their capturing of pertinent COIN experiences and principles include, among others, Frank Kitson, Robert Thompson, and David Galula.

20. Thomas Mockaitis, *British counter-insurgency in the post-Imperial era* (Manchester: Manchester University Press, 1995), 2.

21. Strategy, as considered here, is defined as the identification of the desired political and military end-state in conjunction with the operational goals and tactical methods employed toward the accomplishment of these end-states. "Good" strategy implies the coherence and synergy of ends, ways, and means in conjunction with the effective and efficient use of organization and resources.

22. The levels of war, as considered here, include the strategic, operational, and tactical.

23. Gwynn, *Imperial Policing* (1935), 4-7,14-15; Alderson, "The Validity of British Army Counterinsurgency Doctrine after the War in Iraq 2003-2009," 100-103.

24. Mockaitis, *British counter-insurgency in the post-Imperial era*, 8.

25. Gwynn, *Imperial Policing* (1935), 15, 19; See Chapter VI "Boldness and Vigour: The Essence of Effectively Conducting Such [Small War] Operations" in C. E. Callwell, *Small Wars: Their Principles and Practice*, 3rd ed. (London: Harrison and Sons, 1906), 71-84.

26. Mockaitis, *British counter-insurgency in the post-Imperial era*, 9; Gwynn, *Imperial Policing* (1935), 17-18.

27. *Manual of Military Law*, 1929, War Office, issued by Command of the Army Council, 255.

28. Modern COIN theory accepts that facets of the political, social and economic dynamics of the environment must be rigorously considered and

addressed beyond strictly military considerations. These responsibilities for assessments and policy in these arenas often lie with non-military governmental entities; Mockaitis, *British counter-insurgency in the post-Imperial era*, 1.

29. Gwynn, *Imperial Policing* (1935), 5.

30. Gwynn, *Imperial Policing*, 6.

31. Gwynn, *Imperial Policing*, 5.

32. Charles Townshend, *Britain's Civil Wars: Counterinsurgency in the Twentieth Century* (London: Faber and Faber, 1986), 33.

33. Townshend, *Britain's Civil Wars*, 23.

34. B. C. Denning, "Modern Problems of Guerrilla Warfare," *Army Quarterly and Defence Journal*, 13 (1927): 349.

35. Carl von Clausewitz, *On War*, ed. and trans. by Michael Howard and Peter Paret (Princeton, NJ: Princeton University Press, 1984), 87-88.

36. *Military Lessons of the Arab Rebellion in Palestine, 1936* (War Office, February 1938), 28-37, TNA WO 191/70.

37. Gwynn, *Imperial Policing* (1935), 5.

38. Gwynn, *Imperial Policing*, 5

39. Gwynn, *Imperial Policing*, 13-16.

40. Gwynn, *Imperial Policing*, 103.

41. Gwynn, *Imperial Policing*, 14.

42. Mockaitis, *British counter-insurgency in the post-Imperial era*, 2.

43. Townshend, *Britain's Civil Wars: Counterinsurgency in the Twentieth Century*, 25.

44. The remainder of this quote continues "[such as] Orde Wingate's Night Squads during the Arab Revolt in Palestine," Thomas Mockaitis, *British counter-insurgency in the post-Imperial era* (Manchester University Press: Manchester and New York, 1995), 11.

45. Thomas Mockaitis, *British counter-insurgency in the post-imperial era* (Manchester University Press: Manchester and New York, 1995), 6.

46. Frank Kitson, *Bunch of Five* (London/Boston: Faber and Faber, 1977), 300-301.

Chapter 3
Operational Environment of Palestine and the Grounds for Rebellion

Seeds of Arab Jewish Conflict

Palestine and its governance after the Great War were shaped by Britain's wartime activities of political schemes, vague promises, and military victories.[1] These actions merged with changing dispositions within the international community concerning territorial spoils of war. Together, these greatly affected the dynamics of both the domestic politics that arose as a result of the aspirations of the indigenous peoples as well as the British approach to mandate versus imperial rule. The High Commissioner (HC) for Egypt, Sir Henry McMahon, wrote in 1915 to the Sharif of Mecca, King Hussein, about British support for Arab independence in return for their staging of a revolt.[2] The vagueness of the loosely defined territories to which such support would apply was most certainly intentional in order to allow room for future political maneuvering.

The British diplomat Sir Mark Sykes entered into secret negotiations with the French in 1916 in order to establish spheres of influence should the allies defeat the Ottoman Empire. Palestine, it was agreed, would fall to the British, though the subsequent discovery and release of this information put the British Government on the defensive. The British Secretary of State for Foreign Affairs, Lord Arthur Balfour, wrote of the Cabinet decision in 1917 that "His Majesty's [HM] Government view with favour the establishment in Palestine of a national home for the Jewish people."[3] Then, in 1918, British General Edmund Allenby's exploits during the Sinai and Palestine Campaign resulted in the capture of Ottoman Palestine and an ensuing British rule. The acceptability of long-held practices of appropriating and ruling territory, however, were giving way during this age of nationalism to local demands and international pressure for self-determination.[4]

Soil of the British Mandate for Palestine

The San Remo conference of 1920 entrusted a mandate for Palestine to British tutelage toward independence that took effect in 1923 under the auspices of the League of Nations.[5] The mandate's preamble included the aforementioned phrase of the Balfour declaration along with a subsequent phrase stating that "nothing should be done which might prejudice the civil and religious rights of existing non-Jewish communities in Palestine."[6] While the mandate reinforced the statements contained in the Balfour Declaration, it did not clarify them further even though the concept of a "national home" had no precedent in international law, nor were "civil and religious rights" easily defined. Article Two of the mandate charged Great Britain with "placing the country under such political, administrative and economic conditions as will secure the establishment of the Jewish national home ... and the development of self-governing institutions."[7]

Arab nationalists countered any apparent political gains in favor of Zionist aims to establish a Jewish state in Palestine, as ill-defined as they were, on equally ambiguous legal grounds of their own.[8] These were primarily enumerated as (1) the British wartime assurances to Hussein; (2) the history and overwhelming majority of the Arab population in Palestine; and (3) an article in the Covenant of the League of Nations that implied support for independence to certain communities of the former Ottoman Empire. While it appeared that the Zionist case had the initial political momentum according to the wording in the mandate, the Palestinian Arab Nationalists quickly secured policy statements from the British. These ensured that they would not be subordinated to Jewish rule and that Jewish immigration would be regulated.[9] British initiatives to develop a system of Palestinian self-governance were to be furthered by first instituting a multi-sectarian Legislative Council. This was intended to build the machinery of a unified Arab-Jewish state, but this repeatedly failed due to the intransigence of each community to cooperate with the other.[10] Failing in this, the form of governance closely followed the model of the British Crown Colony and it was placed under the jurisdiction of the Colonial Office.[11]

The British officials that composed the civil government in Palestine were under the overall authority of the HC who also held the title of Commander in Chief. In the discharge of his broad executive and legislature powers, he was aided by Executive and Advisory Councils. A series of departments provided the machinery for administering governance. Administrative Districts were defined as Northern, Southern and Jerusalem Districts for which each was assigned a District Commissioner. The District Commissioners presided over District Officers that could be either British, Arab, or Jewish, and they maintained contact with the local forms of indigenous leadership that were usually represented by *Mukhtars* (village leaders).[12]

Religious, cultural, social, and educational autonomy was increasingly granted to the indigenous population groups along with the freedom to form organizations necessary to administer activities in support of these aims.[13] Many of these organizations progressively provided operational bases for various legal and illegal political and martial activities.[14] The organizations among the Jewish community, however, matured to a greater extent relative to the Arab community, both in their domestic and international functions.[15] The *Yishuv* (settlement) comprised the Jewish population residing in Palestine, and they were largely responsive to the direction provided by a recognized but complicated quasi-government that combined domestic and international Jewish organizations with distinct authorities.[16]

While multiple illegal paramilitary organizations were active among the *Yishuv* throughout this period, the major such organization was known as *Hagana* (The Defense [Force]).[17] On the whole, it was responsive to the centralized leadership's policy decisions such as *havlagah* (restraint) that were intended to maintain an effective system of self-defense against Arab threats, while diplomacy was used to achieve political concessions. This responsiveness occurred despite the fact that it employed a rather decentralized organizational hierarchy largely under the direction of local commanders.[18] *Hagana* was established in 1920 with support by the quasi-government. Among the *Yishuv* it earned the recognition of the people as the underground Jewish defense force representative of the collective needs of the community. There were, however, militant separatist groups and individuals alike that participated in both offensive and reprisal acts of violence. The enduring missions of *Hagana* would prove primarily to be settlement defense, facilitation of illegal immigration, and the maintenance of an all-Jewish para-military capability.[19] Leaders within the Jewish quasi-government encouraged legal paramilitary training of Jews by participation in the British security forces apparatus. Expansion of such forces, to include those with capabilities for offensive operations, would be progressively sought towards the goal of forming the nucleus of a Jewish Army. It was debated among the Jews as to whether a Jewish Army would be a catalyst to or a result of the creation of the hoped-for Jewish state.[20]

The fears and interests of the Arab *fellaheen* (peasant class) were a force of its own that would lead to various forms of support and involvement within the grass-roots element of the Arab militancy of the period. Arab nationalists, elites, and extremist groups would consistently exploit the *fellaheen* as they managed the organization, aims, and direction of the Rebellion in varying degrees and at varying stages throughout the rebellion.[21] Concerning these groups' efforts to further their respective agendas, they were increasingly emboldened in their view of the efficacy of a resort to violence to gain political concessions from the British. This was often done in such a way as to afford deniability.[22] This trend, however, would not appear to gain consistent overwhelming support from the Arab populace, at least not willingly.[23] Coercion and intimidation would be the catalysts that led to the Arab population's rational analysis of their individual security and livelihood interests, to favor the benefits of noncooperation with the government. These terror methods also led to active support or passive noninterference with organized actors of violence.[24] Militant bands eventually formed a sustained military problem for the British and a constant threat to the *Yishuv*. These armed bands of rebels were composed of Arab foreign fighters, religiously inspired militants, and locals motivated by personal vendettas, nationalism or brigandage.[25] These armed bands, however, would continually experience a high degree of factionalism despite attempts to centralize their organization.[26] At times, it would appear that top-down political direction was either ignored or subjugated to the leaders' of the rebel bands use of violent acts as a means for their own ends and interests.[27]

The tortuous but rather consistent British attempts to pursue policies of impartiality and fairness regarding domestic issues in Palestine proved impossible to satisfy either the Arab or Jewish population, let alone both.[28] The difficulties in governing a population so severely divided along two distinct lines of interwoven racial, religious, and political motivations were nevertheless accepted because of the perception of Palestine's strategic interest to the British.[29] The problems of governing Palestine consistently demanded a strong purpose. This purpose was presented as the necessity of Palestine to the defense network of the Near East that in turn was vital to the communications across the Empire. The invocation of the strength of the Empire rested more and more solidly on the monetary and symbolic value of the neighborhood for which Palestine was to "defend," even if only to keep out others that might hold hostile or unfavorable views to British interests. The Suez Canal in Egypt afforded trade and communications to the Empire's holdings in the East, including the "crown jewel" of India. Oil that originated in Iraq was increasingly shipped through the Suez Canal, and in 1935, it then traversed Trans-Jordan and Palestine via pipeline to the port of Haifa. The British Naval, Army, and Air Force bases in Iraq and Egypt were secured by treaty from the time that their independences were granted in 1932 and 1936, but this depended on agreements that needed to be renewed and potentially enforced. Palestine linked the two by securing maritime and overland lines of communication.[30]

Before and during the Arab Rebellion, however, the increasingly worrisome posturing of the Nazis and Fascists in Europe and North Africa would often eclipse the internal concerns taking place in this "vital" British interest of Palestine.[31] Communications between the senior British Army commander in Palestine and the Chief of the Imperial General Staff shed some insight into how Palestine's troubles would be overshadowed by the gathering war clouds. During the height of the 1936 phase of the rebellion, and just after the arrival of a division of troops to assist in countering it, Major General John Dill wrote to Field Marshall Cyril Deverell. He noted, "From what I know of your probable pre-occupations I shall not be surprised to hear that Palestine has become very small beer. I feel quite odd, with only one problem on which to concentrate. But what a problem it is."[32]

Roots of the Arab Rebellion

The Arab Rebellion of 1936 to 1939, itself consisting of multiple phases of intensity and methods of violence, is rightly considered in its broader context to be but a stage in the evolution of the long-standing and burgeoning social, religious, and political frictions at play among the inhabitants of Palestine that were under the rule of the British mandate.[33]

Outbreaks of violence by Arab elements against the Jewish population occurred in 1920, 1921, 1929 and 1933. Violence directed against the British governing authority evolved in frequency and intensity during this period as well. This was a result of a combination of known factors. Increasingly, Arab desires for political independence were stirred, especially with the news of the nationalist surges and achievements in Egypt, Iraq, and Syria. Even more importantly, the Arab fears of impending social upheaval resulting from Jewish immigration and land purchases were turning into a grave anxiety that the trend would not only shatter Palestinian Arabs' Nationalist hopes but lead to eventual subjugation by the Jews.[34]

Meanwhile, Jewish aspirations for Palestine to become the refuge for world Jewry were extremely heightened in their experience of rising anti-Semitism and persecution in Europe. This was heavily experienced in Poland but epitomized by the events accompanying the rise of Adolf Hitler and the Nazi party in Germany from 1933 onward. As a result, Jewish immigration into Palestine from 1932 to 1935 grew exponentially both legally and illegally.[35] After a Jewish arms-smuggling operation was exposed and a highly publicized Palestinian "freedom fighter," Sheikh 'Izz al'Din al-Qassam, was killed in a clash with security forces in 1935, the tensions in Palestine were nearing the crisis point. The arrival of 1936 brought not only an economic crisis and another failure to establish a Legislative Council in Palestine, but it also brought ever-heightening anxieties and perceived opportunities in a seemingly imminent European War.[36] The stage was set for a cascading chain of events that would crystallize into the first phase of the Arab Rebellion and encompass most of the remainder of 1936.

Notes

1. For an overview of the British in the Middle East during this period, specifically from 1914 to 1922, see David Fromkin, *A Peace to End All Peace* (New York: Henry Holt and Company, 1989).

2. McMahon later stated that "it was not intended by me in giving this pledge to King Hussein to include Palestine in the area in which Arab independence was promised" and that he "had every reason to believe at the time that the fact that Palestine was not included in my pledge was well understood by King Hussein." See letter to the editor of *The Times* from A. Henry McMahon, 23 July 1937, LHC 15/5/297. For a contextual overview of this period see J. C. Hurewitz, *The Struggle for Palestine* (New York: Greenwood Press, 1968), 17-20; and Christopher Sykes, *Crossroads to Israel: 1917-1948* (Bloomington, IN: Indiana University Press, 1973), 3-40.

3. Balfour later admitted that "Our policy may fail. I do not deny that this is an adventure." See Sykes, *Crossroads to Israel: 1917-1948* (Bloomington, IN: Indiana University Press, 19733-4), 3-4, 7.

4. Sykes, *Cossroads to Israel: 1917-1948*, 10; Hurewitz, *The Struggle for Palestine* (New York: Greenwood Press, 1968), 17.

5. For an overview of the mandate and a reference for its original documents, see The Mandate for Palestine as prepared by The Division of Near Eastern Affairs for the US Department of State in 1927, reprinted as The Palestine Mandate (Documentary Publications; Salisbury, NC, 1977).

6. Hurewitz, *The Struggle for Palestine*, 17-18.

7. Hurewitz, *The Struggle for Palestine*, 18-19.

8. For a comprehensive understanding of Zionism, see Howard Sachar, *A History of Israel: From the Rise of Zionism to Our Time*, 2nd ed. (New York: Alfred A. Knopf, 2003); Sykes, *Crossroads to Israel: 1917-1948*, 13. Here, "Zionism" refers to the movement standing for the establishment of a Jewish state in Palestine.

9. George Antonius, *The Arab Awakening: The Story of the Arab National Movement* (Safety Harbor: Simon Publications, 2001), 390-391; Hurewitz, *The Struggle for Palestine*, 18-23.

10. War Office, Palestine: Information for Commanders of Reinforcing Troops, TNA WO 33/1436.

11. Hurewitz, *The Struggle for Palestine*, 23.

12. Hurewitz, *The Struggle for Palestine*, 23; "Palestine: Information for Commanders of Reinforcing Troops," 7 September 1936, TNA WO 33/1436; H. J. Simson, *British Rule, and Rebellion*, (Edinburgh: William Blackwood & Sons Ltd., 1937), 161-163.

13. Hurewitz, *The Struggle for Palestine*, 24, 38-63.

14. Simson, *British Rule, and Rebellion*, 164-168.

15. For an extensive overview of the social and political organization of the Arab and Jewish populations, see Hurewitz, The Struggle for Palestine, 33-63.

16. Hurewitz, *The Struggle for Palestine*, 38-42.

17. *Hagana* was known to exist and to possess unauthorized weapons, but the enforcement of the British policy was generally lax. This was largely due to the recognized need of the *Yishuv* to protect itself in conjunction with the inability of the official security forces to provide protection with such a low density of forces to cover widely dispersed settlements.

18. History of the Disturbances in Palestine 1936-1939: Notes on Operations in Palestine Between November 1937 & December 1939, 3, TNA WO 191/88; Hurewitz, *The Struggle for Palestine*, 24; Uri Ben-Eliezer, *The Making of Israeli Militarism* (Bloomington, IN: Indiana University Press, 1998), 3; Yehoshua Porath, *The Palestinian Arab National Movement: From Riots to Rebellion, Volume Two: 1929-1939* (London: Frank Cass and Company Limited, 1977), 70.

19. David Ben-Gurion. "We Defend Ourselves – Illegal Immigration The Strongest Weapon," Jewish Observer and Middle East Review, 13 September 1963, LH 15/5/311.

20. Ben-Eliezer, *The Making of Israeli Militarism*, 3, 19-21. For an insider account on the history and deliberations on policy for the *Haganah*, see the series of articles written by David Ben-Gurion in 1963-64, especially, David Ben-Gurion, "Britain's Contribution to Arming the Hagana," Jewish Observer and Middle East Review, 20 September 1963, LH 15/5/311; Hurewitz, *The Struggle for Palestine*, 24.

21. See Tom Bowden, *The Breakdown of Public Security: The Case of Ireland 1916-1921* and *Palestine 1936-1939* (London: Sage Publications, 1977), 178-192, where he describes the rebellion as "a racial, religious, colonial, familial and peasant struggle intermingled." For one of the most extensively researched works on the period drawing from English, Arabic and Hebrew sources, see Yehoshua Porath, *The Palestinian Arab National Movement: From Riots to Rebellion, Volume Two: 1929-1939*, 162-273.

22. Hurewitz, *The Struggle for Palestine*, 24.

23. Charles Gwynn, *Imperial Policing* (London: Macmillan and Co., 1939), 365-372, as posted in the 2004 Internet edition, http://www.combatreform.org/PENTOMICARMYAGAIN/imperialpolicing.htm; 51-63, 67; Simson, *British Rule, and Rebellion*, 165-168; Military Lessons of the Arab Rebellion in Palestine, 1936 (War Office, February 1938), 29, TNA WO 191/70; See George Antonius, *The Arab Awakening*, 405-409, for the view that the Arab rebellion was manned and persisted consistently by the grievances and nationalist ideals of the Arab peasant class.

24. Bowden, *The Breakdown of Public Security: The Case of Ireland 1916-1921 and Palestine 1936-1939*, 179-182; Gwynn, *Imperial Policing (1939)*, 389-390; Porath, *The Palestinian Arab National Movement: From Riots to Rebellion, Volume Two: 1929-1939*, 177-178, 187, 190.

25. Porath, *The Palestinian Arab National Movement: From Riots to Rebellion, Volume Two: 1929-1939*, 181, 183, 185, 188-189, 194.

26. Porath, *The Palestinian Arab National Movement*, 182, 191-193, 300-301. For one of the few collections and analysis of captured Arab rebel documents,

see Ya'acov Shimoni, and Ezra Danon, Documents and Portraits from the Records of the Arab Gangs in the Arab Revolt, 1936-1939 (Jerusalem; Magnes Press, 1981). A translated copy can be found at TBL M2313.

27. One of many such periodic assessments by the British was recorded as: "the campaign of violence... appears to have broken away entirely from the control of the Higher Arab Committee and is now in the hands of irresponsible extremists" as stated in Palestine: Information for Commanders of Reinforcing Troops, 7 September 1936, TNA WO 33/1436; See the War Office release in January 1939 for an overview of the issues discussed in this paragraph at that time, LH 15/3/71; Bowden, *The Breakdown of Public Security: The Case of Ireland 1916-1921 and Palestine 1936-1939*, 192-204.

28. It should be noted, however, that these internal policies were heavily influenced by the government's accounting for how they might resonate with the greater Arab and Muslim world, for which British interests were closely tied. Sykes, *Crossroads to Israel: 1917-1948*, 20; Hurewitz, *The Struggle for Palestine*, 23-24.

29. For the strategic interest of Palestine as enumerated by the Committee on Palestine in a report for the Colonial Office as of April 1939, see TNA CO 733/410/11.

30. Hurewitz, *The Struggle for Palestine*, 21, 25-26; Sykes. *Crossroads to Israel: 1917-1948*, 9; See also Herbert Sidebotham, *British Imperial Interests in Palestine* (Letchworth; The Garden City Press Ltd., 1937), 2, LH 15/5/299, for the text of his memorandum submitted to the Royal Commission headed by Lord Peel, wherein he states "It is no longer necessary to stress the Imperial interest of Great Britain in Palestine." Mr. Sidebotham was sympathetic to Zionism, but the statement is telling of the almost axiomatic case he presents as it comes from "the leading political journalist of his time" according to Hurewitz.

31. Winston Churchill, *Step By Step: 1936-1939* (London: Thornton Butterworth Ltd, 1939), 290.

32. Letter from Major General John Dill to Field Marshall Cyril Deverell, 22 September 1936, LHC Dill Collection 2/9, Document 5a, 3.

33. See the official History of the Disturbances in Palestine 1936-1939: Notes on Operations in Palestine Between November 1937 & December 1939, TNA WO 191/88.

34. Simson, *British Rule, and Rebellion*, 160; Porath, *The Palestinian Arab National Movement: From Riots to Rebellion, Volume Two: 1929-1939*, 140.

35. Porath, *The Palestinian Arab National Movement: From Riots to Rebellion, Volume Two: 1929-1939, 39-40*, 133-140; Sykes, *Crossroads to Israel: 1917-1948*, 20; Hurewitz, *The Struggle for Palestine*, 135-138, 144.

36. Porath, T*he Palestinian Arab National Movement: From Riots to Rebellion, Volume Two: 1929-1939*, 140-141, 143-159.

Chapter 4
The Arab Rebellion and Internal Security in Palestine

April 1936—Breakdown of Public Security

In mid-April of 1936, the unfortunate but rather ordinary sequence of inter-ethnic violence escalated beyond the typical spate of limited attack and reprisal. The news of murder and its accompanying rumors spread throughout Palestine, leading to riots in the major cities. A flurry of Arab political activity at all levels over the following days led to a breakthrough in the deadlock that had heretofore prevented a unified Arab political front with nationalist goals. A Higher Arab Committee was formed. A general strike was decreed for Arab workers while political demands were put forth to the government to include a cessation of Jewish immigration and land purchases as well as the establishment of a representative government. These were quickly followed by calls to the Arab public for civil disobedience while sporadic acts of violence and sabotage against both the Jews and the government started to the take the shape of an organized campaign of violence. Arson, sniping, bombing, sabotage of infrastructure, and attacks on motor vehicles were beginning to establish themselves as fundamental elements of the rebellion within the first month. The volume of these incidents prompted the civil government to send requests for military reinforcements. The British Government declared that a Royal Commission would proceed to Palestine in order to investigate Arab political grievances. The announcement came with the stipulation that it would only proceed to Palestine after order was restored.[1]

May to June 1936—Action and Reaction

As the first military reinforcements were arriving in May to undertake security and defensive operations, the rebellion was spreading from the cities to the rural areas. The formation of armed bands prompted further calls for reinforcements by the civil government. The reinforcements arrived piecemeal in response to the gradual escalations and then dispersed into small protective details throughout the country acting "in aid to the civil power." They had neither the concentrated strength nor the authority for providing offensive action.

By mid-June the smuggling of arms and foreign fighters from Iraq and Syria through Jordan had swelled some of the gangs' operational strengths to between 50 and 70 fighters. These numbers led to an increase in the frequency and audacity of their attacks while they gained valuable experience through experimentation in their use of guerrilla tactics. Another emerging trend that would mark the rebellion revealed itself in the rebels' employment of an organized and persistent propaganda campaign along with the use of civil and legal complaints against the security forces.

These actions heightened the political sensitivities among the British public and government toward the counter-rebellion campaign. In turn, the propaganda and complaints were catalysts that emplaced limitations and restrictions on the security forces' actions and employment. In Palestine, legal challenges from Palestinian Arabs exposed a weakness in the cooperation of the legal apparatus to enforce the severe punishments authorized through a series of defense and emergency regulations.[2]

As engagements between HM Forces and the bands became a regular occurrence, another trend emerged: The initiative and surprise was with the armed gangs of rebels. Despite (or rather because of) the firepower that HM Forces were able to bring to bear, the Arab guerrillas sought to avoid decisive engagements and were successful in choosing the battle site and initiating contact more often than not. Engagements often took the form of ambushes. After ambushing a motorized convoy in a location chosen for its tactical advantage, the rebel gangs were able to retreat with at least a psychological victory given the most probable scenarios that would play themselves out after the initial engagement. If the mission of a convoy required haste, then its haphazard returning of fire and continuing of mission led to the disadvantages of inevitably inaccurate fire from the vehicles as well as the perception of having fled the battlefield. If HM Forces were to be dismounted for counterattack, not only were they now exposed in a gunfight against covered and concealed guerillas, but the lightly clad and armed rebels who held the advantage in knowledge and navigation of the terrain could disperse quickly. The rebels could even "transform" themselves into villagers or shepherds to escape their pursuers only to return later to claim the battlefield. The tendency for the rebels to stage such attacks with the approach of dusk or at night took away the advantage that airpower was discovered to bring to the fight in maintaining contact once the elusive rebels were found (or rather exposed themselves) and engaged.[3]

The armed bands would pose a constant problem in their persistent elusiveness and maintenance of guerrilla capabilities. Throughout the rebellion, the rebels' emphasis on the types of guerrilla operations to be conducted would change to both maximize the frustration of the security forces' measures taken against them and to preserve their force.[4] The "warrior ethos" of the rebels never earned the respect of HM Forces on account of the fact they would not stand to fight and that their overall effectiveness in guerrilla warfare would remain highly dependent on individual bands' experience and leadership. Rebel attempts to "professionalize" their force, however, would emerge.[5] Foreign fighters and guerrilla leadership, funding, and "full-time" Palestinian rebels would progressively emerge. A guerrilla warfare doctrine would also emerge, named the *Damascus F.S.R.* (Field Service Regulations), and it would be published in pamphlet form.[6]

July to August 1936—Strengths and Weaknesses

In July and August, the violence continued unabated. The close of the Abyssinian War allowed the release of British troops from Egypt and Malta for duty in Palestine. For the first time, the military was able to field sufficient forces capable of conducting large sweeps for village searches and, if encountered, to bring the armed bands to battle. These actions proved to be largely unsuccessful. Between poor operational security, the leak of information on security operations from Arab governmental employees, and the time and distance necessary for units to travel, in conjunction with the "eyes" of the rebels or rebel informants, the rebels would more often than not enjoy ample warning of HM Forces' moves.[7] In August, an ex-Iraqi and Syrian Military Officer, Fawzi al-Quwuqji, infiltrated into Palestine with experienced guerrilla fighters and leaders. Meanwhile, the latest of attempts at political mediation failed despite the civil government's facilitation of foreign Arab officials to act as interlocutors.[8]

At the outset of the rebellion, the government's security forces in Palestine included a garrison of military forces that included two infantry battalions, more than a squadron of the Royal Air Force and a Royal Air Force company of armored cars. These would grow to almost two full divisions in six months. Air Vice Marshal R.E.C. Peirse of the Royal Air Force commanded the military forces, but he did so as the military adviser to HC Arthur Wauchope. Therefore, the military acted under the authority and direction of the HC. The Trans-Jordan Frontier Force operated in eastern Palestine along the Jordan River Valley for frontier security under the direction of the HC.[9] The Palestine Police consisted of nearly 3,000 policemen to include about 750 British Officers and other ranks in conjunction with about 1750 Arabs and 375 Jews. The police were organized under the civil government with an inspector general as their senior representative under the authority and direction of the HC.[10]

Auxiliaries to the police were employed for duties ranging from drivers, protection of infrastructure, and reinforcements to the police force. They were expanded during the first six months of the rebellion to number around 3,500 by September. The overwhelming majority of these auxiliaries, referred to as "supernumeraries," were Jewish. These Jewish supernumeraries were primarily employed as security guards for the defense of Jewish settlements against Arab attacks.[11] This force would continue to expand throughout the rebellion owing to their increased need in conjunction with shortages of other security forces to fill this role. Another factor for this growth was the Jewish lobbying for increased capability to protect the *Yishuv*. The largely Jewish character of this force created a heightened political sensitivity to their numbers and employment throughout the rebellion due to their impact on Arab sensibilities.[12]

The military mission was conducted "in aid to the civil power," therefore the Palestine Police were expected to take the lead in restoration of order.[13] A description of the time stated that "its armament and training are much more nearly military than is usual and resemble those of Gendarmerie."[14] Under the direction of the HC, the military was dispersed in order to conduct protective duties, secure lines of communication, and provide security details for convoys. The military was generally employed to conduct any security activity necessary to help the police force maximize its manpower for priority missions. This arrangement often resulted in military personnel executing "police" duties while the police conducted military-style operations.[15] The traditional British security emphasis on the primacy of the police has many roots, but one of the police's primary practical reasons for being pushed into the lead when countering rebellion was the capability for obtaining information. The police worked among the people and held the language ability necessary to perform this function, but there were issues developing in Palestine that prevented this asset from meeting its expectations.[16] Already divided loyalties among the Arabs of the Palestine Police were further widened as a result of the progressively intensive campaign of Arab-on-Arab coercion and terror to enforce "loyalty" to the cause. Cracks in the police were beginning to show as early as June.[17] In the absence of martial law, powers had to be conferred upon the military to include those of search, arrest, and the imposition of collective fines.[18]

Fall 1936 to Spring 1937
Policy and Subwar

Despite requests from the military for the instatement of martial law and the implementation of "repressive measures," the government's policy decision up to this point was one of "endeavouring to protect life and property without adopting repressive measures."[19] This policy would continue until September when the military forces required to execute a new policy were en route to employ "intensive measures designed to crush the resistance."[20] With no end of the violence in sight, this change in policy was prompted by an acknowledgment among British Government officials that their current policy was failing in its near-term expectations for restoring order. The HC's approach to the policy thus far was driven largely by considerations of the policy's effects toward the future restoration of peace. His intention was to prevent the arousal of unnecessary bitterness toward the government. It was his hope that the civil government could resume its work to fulfill the mandate charter with the smallest degree of setbacks post-rebellion. He would later state to General Dill, the new General Officer Commanding (GOC) of the two divisions now employed there, that sterner measures would also have been a political liability if the Royal Commission were to report that the Arab grievances were well founded.[21]

Martial law was initially approved in London, but ensuing governmental deliberations led to the withdrawal of the authorization. In its stead, specific authority was to be delegated to the military for making regulations on security issues. The emergency regulations would take time to be developed due to their requirements to be spelled out in detail.[22] Before these measures were able to be implemented, though, the Higher Arab Committee called off the strike and the violence. This was a result of the threat of martial law, the influx of troops, the mediation of foreign Arab kings, and the fact that the Arab population had suffered significant financial loss. These developments coincided with the impending commencement of the citrus harvest that was a major source of employment and income for the *fellaheen*.[23]

General Dill was frustrated with the security strategy and he voiced his criticisms toward the limitations imposed on his military options for countering the rebellion.[24] Internally, he issued a statement to the troops under his command commending them for their efforts that had led to the waning of the rebellion "in spite of hampering and difficult circumstances." This reference clearly pointed to policy limitations, as the publication of these remarks in the local press were immediately prohibited on order of the HC.[25] In communications with the War Office, Dill criticized the effects of a purely defensive strategy and expressed his opinions on the failure to instate martial law. It was his "impression that HM Government's intention had not been carried out … " and that "an opportunity had been missed of re-establishing British authority."[26] Dill witnessed the denial of his recommendations to the HC to apprehend the leader of the Higher Arab Committee as well as the cancellation of an operation that he had planned to strike at the armed Arab gangs that were still in existence. He further expressed his concerns for the likelihood of a renewed rebellion, owing to the facts that the Arab political and military organizations maintained their capabilities for renewing acts of violence.[27] In a memorandum to the HC, Dill points out that:

> Any failure to take prompt measures in the face of organized rebellion, including the declaration of Martial Law, will always lead to waste of effort and the ultimate necessity of having to provide more and more reinforcements to cope with the situation. This is the main lesson of the recent rebellion when a policy of forbearance and particularly a desire not to leave bitterness prevented the early declaration of Martial Law and led to greater and greater forces being required. I am sure you will agree that such a policy cannot be followed in the face of a fresh rebellion. In any case it is a policy which it would be the duty of any commander to resist.[28]

While Dill's opinions and words were communicated strongly as he executed his duties as GOC in Palestine and military adviser to the HC, they appear to be consistently nuanced in appropriateness for both his audience and the channels through which he exercised his influence. Elsewhere within the military, the policy and its restrictions drew criticism that can only be described as scathing.[29] The War Office publication titled *Military Lessons of the Arab Rebellion in Palestine, 1936* was published in early 1938 and devoted seven pages to such criticisms. Its critical evaluations were against (1) the policy of "conciliation" that was pursued versus the policy of "repression" that was preferred; (2) the civil government's failure to employ effective counter-propaganda; and (3) the policy's detrimental effects on the conduct of military operations. Criticisms of the government's policy were also present in the book written by H.J. Simson, a serving British officer in Palestine in 1936.

Simson first introduced the concept of subwar, which he identified as rising in prominence since World War I and epitomized in both Northern Ireland and in Palestine. He defined subwar as an insurgency employing guerrilla warfare in combination with propaganda against the government, terrorism to control the population and neutralize the police, and secret organizations to control and/or exploit the complex collage of actors, motivations, and incidents toward the achievement of political goals.[30] Simson acknowledged the political difficulties in supporting the means necessary to defeat subwar as well as the challenges to implementing an effective form of martial law. He did not propose, however, that this emerging form of war required a total departure from the traditional military methods needed to quell rebellion. He asserted that prompt use of force against the subversive organization and better cooperation between the civil, military, police, and legal organizations were imperative for an effective, synergistic, and comprehensive strategy to prevail over such an insurgency.[31] He identified the government's ineptitudes in understanding this form of rebellion and establishing effective policies to defeat it.[32] He declares that "The Army in particular gains wide experience in constant contact with rebellion . . . [,] But the policy governing its action . . . [is] controlled by amateurs."[33]

Wingate's Entrance into Theater

The influx of troops into Palestine from the military surge in September of 1936 brought about a restructuring of the military organization with the now two divisions in country. The experienced units already in Palestine were consolidated under the 5th Division in the North due to the higher levels of rebel activity there. The newly arrived division was given an Area of Operations (AO) in the South.[34] With the reorganization of forces, the staff of the 5th Division Headquarters in Haifa was expanded. Orde Wingate was assigned as a General Staff Officer, Grade 3 (Captain), Intelligence.[35] He would quickly set about learning the contemporary history and modern politics of Palestine which would build upon his select knowledge of its ancient history gained through the reading of the Bible and his Christian faith.[36] He also began learning Hebrew, which would distinguish him as one of the few officers to read and speak the three official languages of Palestine.[37]

A few months later Wingate would be transferred to an intelligence officer position within the corps General Headquarters in Jerusalem. During his initial months in Haifa, however, his endeavors to understand the situation would have already led him to accept a staunch pro-Zionist position. This was on the whole counter to the general attitudes within the British civil administration and military.[38] He revealed his early (and what would prove to be long) held opinions on a few points of interest as early as January 1937 in a letter to his "Cousin Rex" (Sir Reginald Wingate, the accomplished British general and administrator in Egypt and the Sudan). Orde Wingate recognized the military potential of the Jews for use in countering the Arab rebellion. He also noted the idea's merits in allowing for the British Military to treat Palestine as an economy-of-force mission within the greater Empire. Wingate criticized the civil administration, the civil administrators themselves, and the policies undertaken thus far in Palestine. He particularly noted his perception of the "anti-Jew[ish]" sentiment of the Palestine Administration.[39] He would later comment on his perception of the anti-Jewish sentiment within the military as well. The attitudes within the military appear to have been less overtly pro-Arab than those of the Colonial and Foreign Offices, but they could still be considered as such in general.[40] The strength of Wingate's Zionist opinions, however, would easily interpret anything less than his extremes to fall into that category; therefore, his writings refer to them as such. There were pro-Zionist voices within the political and military realms, but these were the minority.

The Colonial and Foreign Offices' deep apprehension for potential offenses to Arab and Muslim sensitivities was rooted in practical concerns for the empire that included large swaths of this ethnicity and religion. The military considerations included practical concern over Arab and Muslim sensitivities because of the potential effects on the Arab components of the security forces within Palestine. It must also be remembered that there was a longstanding and widely accepted practice in the British Military thought of the day to classify races as "martial" and "non-martial." The Jews had long been considered the latter while the Palestinian Arabs were a step away from the former. For the Jews, this meant that their military utility to the British was implicitly recognized as questionable at best. As for the Palestinian Arabs, they did not fit neatly into the Martial and Non-Martial theoretical paradigm. The British Army's experience with Arabs and Muslims most certainly contributed to a familiarity and comfort level with their employment; however, the "fighting" prowess of Palestinian Arabs would repeatedly be called into question whether acting as friend or foe. The association of Palestinian Arabs' with the Bedouin was likely a psychological contributor to those in the British Military who did tend to lean towards a pro-Arab bias. The Bedouin were a highly romanticized martial race in general British opinion; especially given the drama and publicity that was taking place during this time surrounding T. E. Lawrence's exploits during World War I and his recent death. While Wingate was in fact a distant relative to Lawrence, he would vociferously point out the differences in their military thought and operational practice despite, or rather because of, the temptation of many to draw comparisons. Wingate's forceful contradistinction could very well have been more of a function of Zionist versus Arab bias than the argumentation that he employed, but this is unclear.[41]

Wingate would establish many local contacts during his tenure in Palestine, and got off to a quick start. These were primarily with influential Jewish personalities associated with either Jewish political organizations or *Hagana*. These acquaintances included such figures as Emmanuel Wilenski, Eliahu Golomb, Abba Eban, Moshe Shertok and David Ben-Gurion. His Arab acquaintances also included men of such prominence as George Antonius.[42] Wingate also met and quickly established a close relationship with Chaim Weizmann, one of the principal Zionist leaders of the era. This particular introduction was inadvertently initiated by Sir Reginald Wingate when he arranged for Orde Wingate to meet the HC. The HC hosted a dinner party that both Wingate and Weizmann attended.[43] Orde Wingate's adept use of "patrons" in conjunction with his experiences in the efficacy of influencing those who were influential, were at this point an already developing skill.[44] Though there were explicit instructions that British officials were not to become involved in Palestinian politics, this appears to have been widely ignored in practice. Wingate would stand out, however, not only because his circles included those in positions of such great influence but also because they were largely Jewish instead of Arab.[45] His ability to make a quick and deep impression on those he met would be a trait recounted by numerous military and political notables from this point in his career and forward.[46]

A "Loaded" Spring

Throughout the winter of 1936 and into the spring of 1937, Lieutenant General Dill sought to influence and clarify both policy and civil-military relations for the anticipated recrudescence of violence. He strongly advocated the instatement of martial law. As he continually fell short in this endeavor, he simultaneously sought to maximize the effects of his force within the constraints of the policies.[47] Meanwhile, the Royal Commission finished its hearings and collection of evidence in Palestine in January of 1937, but its findings would not be released until July. During this period, the garrison was reduced to six battalions, emergency powers for both the police and the military were refined (though with much difficulty), and the violence remained relatively abated in anxious anticipation of the Royal Commission's Report.[48] The tensions remained high while the organizations and capabilities for further rebellion remained intact. This was due in part to the intervention of the Foreign Office in curbing the military's recommendations to disarm the population. This intervention was initiated out of fear that such a move would "endanger the peaceful settlement which now seems to be in sight." The military also harbored concerns about pursuing a policy of disarmament, but their argument followed a very different line. While disarmament was believed necessary for an enduring peace, they would not recommend such a move without the authorities (i.e. martial law) and the troops available to properly execute and enforce it.[49]

Partition Plan and "Palliatives"

The Royal Commission's Report declared the mandate unworkable due to the political impasse of the Arab and Jewish political demands. Therefore, a partition scheme was recommended to create independent Arab and Jewish states with British interests secured by privileged treaties. A narrow British zone of control would encompass Jerusalem and a strip of land connecting it to the Mediterranean as well as isolated ports in Haifa and Aqabah.[50] These primary findings were partially unacceptable to the Jews based on their overriding concern that Palestine be sufficiently large enough to provide a place of refuge for persecuted Jewry worldwide. The findings were wholly unacceptable to the Arabs as they reiterated their initial political demands. Attention shifted to the "palliatives" offered by the Royal Commission that were provided as alternatives if its primary recommendations proved unacceptable, though these were prescribed as treatment for symptoms and therefore not intended to be a cure. These included addressing the rates of Jewish immigration as well as recommendations for the handling of the security situation. An overhaul of the Palestine Police was one such recommendation among the report's criticisms of the policies and actions pursued thus far towards gaining control of the security situation.[51]

Fall 1937 to Spring 1938

Severe Measures

Acts of violence were increasingly renewed with vigor over the course of the remainder of 1937. The violence directed against the British Government was preceded by growing Arab on Arab terrorism with occasional Jewish reprisal attacks for Arab assaults against the *Yishuv*. After the assassination of a District Commissioner in early September, the threats of severe policies were acted upon.[52] Suspect Arab political leadership was targeted for arrest in October resulting in the detention, deportation, or dispersal of many rebel leaders and supporters to include the Mufti himself. He escaped the country to eventually set up a headquarters in Syria, around which many Arab political and militant dissidents from Palestine would coalesce. From within and without, preparations were made for continuing the rebellion. The Mufti continued to exert influence over the armed bands that enjoyed a renewed influx of foreign fighters as well as a surge of Arab Palestinians. These militant rebels harbored a variety of motivations that included repaying blood feuds, personal profit and racketeering, and carrying on the struggle as Arab Nationalist Freedom Fighters. Throughout the fall and winter, the establishment of military courts streamlined the efficiency of prosecuting violators of the revised laws that were brought about through emergency powers. The two Brigades of military forces also began offensive operations against the armed bands.[53]

General Wavell replaced Dill as the GOC in September of 1937. In October, Sir Harold MacMichael was chosen to replace Wauchope as the HC but it would not be until February of 1938 before the transition would occur. It was not only determined that Wauchope was representative of a policy that had proved too lenient, but that his former life of being a British Military Officer was more of a hindrance than a help. The dynamic of civil-military relations relied upon the HC's respect for military expertise for two important functions. The first of which concerned the military's duty to advise the civil government in its handling of the security situation. The second concerned the HC's capacity to transfer powers from the civil to military spheres.[54]

The issue of declaring martial law was fully debated by the British Cabinet but it was decided that it would not be implemented in Palestine. The new HC would prove much more willing to support a more severe line however, especially after having taken account of the multitude of criticisms directed at the policies taken thus far.[55] "Military control" was the hybrid legal state that undergirded the authority of the military to take action from November of 1937 until December of 1939. It would not be until late in 1938, however, that the legal infrastructure would be built and the forces available to enforce it would be able to effectively exploit the more severe authorities. These authorities were less than those offered under martial law, but they allowed for matters of public security to be handed over and made the overall responsibility of the GOC. This arrangement included powers that were delegable to Military Area Commanders thereby allowing them to publish area-specific emergency regulations on all issues relating to security.[56]

Military Actions and Police Reform

Shaping operations for military offensives included both the building of roads along the frontiers to enable access by mobile forces as well as measures taken in an effort to separate the rebels from the population. The latter was primarily achieved through the use of the military for village occupation in conjunction with the use of punitive actions against both individuals and communities for rebel activity.[57] Throughout the rebellion, the rebel bands would consistently concentrate themselves most heavily in the North due to the advantages afforded by the hilly terrain. The Royal Commission had recommended this area of northern Palestine to be part of the Jewish state under partition. This resulted in further motivation for the Arabs that resided there to rebel. The area fell within the 16th Infantry Brigade's AO under the Command of Brigadier General Sir John Evetts. The combination of village occupation by HM Forces and an experiment by the rebel leaders to fully utilize the numbers of fighters available to them, led to the mustering of large rebel bands that operated in the countryside throughout this area. Repeated engagements took place throughout the winter and into the spring of 1938, in which British Forces employed tactical formations that were developed for frontier warfare. These were composed of multiple mobile columns acting in concert with each other and with the Royal Air Force. This resulted in both the rebel bands' attrition and their realization that employment of such large formations (often numbering in the hundreds) were clearly to their military disadvantage.[58]

Meanwhile, the Royal Commission's recommendation for an overhaul of the Palestine Police led to the hire of one of the most respected police administrators of the time, Sir Charles Tegart. He was brought in to both assess and make recommendations for the reformation of the Palestine Police.[59] Having arrived in the fall of 1937, he made a series of recommendations over his several-month stay that were being reviewed and successively implemented beginning in early 1938.[60] Of note were Tegart's recommendations to (1) reorganize the Criminal Investigation Department for better intelligence collection; (2) address his concern over the frontier units' lack of patrolling at night; (3) build a fence across the Northern frontier; and (4) stand up a Rural Mounted Police Unit as a hard-hitting mobile paramilitary force designed to counter the rebel gangs.[61] While the execution of basic police duties were overwhelming by simple virtue of the amount of work to be done in correcting the security situation, the armed bands would prove themselves to be a constant and formidable threat to the police throughout 1938. Rebel attacks on Police Stations would at times result in their being completely overrun and the surrounding areas falling under rebel control, and their intimidation of police officers and their families was increasingly effective.[62]

Jewish Security Forces, Policy, and Wingate

The rebel capability of massing to attack during this period was a serious threat, not only to the smaller police outposts that Tegart had recommended to be consolidated for better protection, but to the *Yishuv* settlements as well. As of January 1938, the Jewish supernumeraries being used for settlement defense had been expanded to number about 5,000. Though only 1,000 of these supernumeraries were on the books as being paid, armed, and employed fulltime, all but 700 of the remaining supernumeraries were on call for emergencies with arms that were issued and stored for emergency defense.[63] The Jewish strategy of planned rural settlement through the successive establishment of Jewish villages was a largely successful and continuous aim throughout the whole of the Arab rebellion. These settlements were intended to display their resolution in the face of Arab terror as well as to pre-position the Jews for a more favorable partition settlement through both reinforcement and expansion of the areas of their population densities.[64]

In addition to the underground Jewish security apparatus that included intelligence and defense units, Jewish requests were increasingly made throughout the rebellion for a more permanent and robust integration of Jews into the British security forces apparatus in Palestine.[65] In 1936, British policy set conditions such as the dismantlement of *Hagana* before they were willing to accede to such requests. According to Ben-Gurion, this condition was dropped in no small part due to "pressure from the Military (which did not always support the pro-Arab tendencies of the Administration and understood the difference between the Arab gangs and the *Hagana*)".[66] A progressive tendency for the British Government to lessen the restrictions placed on the employment of supernumeraries throughout the Arab Rebellion did take place.[67] It was never extensive enough, however, to satisfy an increasingly loud Jewish voice for such units, though the *Yishuv* and its leadership would never unanimously agree on the issue. The requests for expansion of the use of Jews in the security forces especially called for units or sub-units to be composed of either entirely Jewish personnel or a combination of Jewish Soldiers and Officers with British Officers. British security forces that were made up in whole or part by indigenous personnel were a long tradition of British Military practice. Both the region and Palestine itself saw the use of such units to include the Arab Legion in Trans-Jordan and the Trans-Jordan Frontier Force, though they were both of an overwhelmingly Arab character.[68]

Wingate himself would hail from this tradition having commanded a Sudanese Defense Force *Idara* (tactical unit roughly equivalent to an oversized light infantry company) comprised of about 300 indigenous Sudanese Soldiers. He gained what would prove to be valuable experimentation and practice in tracking down and bringing gangs of poachers to action.[69] It should not be surprising or odd, therefore, given his conviction in the military potential of Jews as an indigenous population group that he would see the potential for such a unit being formed. Considering his own qualifications in experience and language (as well as in his sympathies and determination), it is also not surprising that he would see the potential in his being chosen to lead such an organization. He stated his desire to do so in his letter to Sir Reginald Wingate as early as January of 1937. He stated that "I'd sooner be raising a Jewish Brigade (under Govt.!) to defend our interests in the coming war!"[70] Shortly thereafter in May, and on no other authority than his own, he would formally plant the seed in Weizmann's mind. In Wingate's recognition of the "paramount importance to look far ahead", he would communicate through a letter to Weizmann both the potential of "the formation of a Jewish Palestine Defence Force" and his desire to lead it.[71] Wingate duly recounted his own qualifications for such a position and requested further communication about the subject, though no written records exist for what surely remained to be discussed discretely and in person.[72]

The concept for a Jewish Military Force was one that was often officially discussed, and it would continue to be discussed throughout the Arab Rebellion and into World War II.[73] In late 1937 and early 1938, official deliberations over such a force were spurred on by a Jewish request and they led to talks between the GOC, the HC and the Colonial Office. The request was not recommended or accepted at the time due, in the words of Lieutenant General Sir Robert Haining, to "political objections" considered to "rest on the fact that we are the mandatory power, endeavoring to hold a nice balance between two antagonistic races. ..."[74] It was admitted that "the scheme for forming a Jewish unit is, for the present at any rate, inopportune ..." but that "this question will crop up again later."[75] The HC stated that "If it were not for political considerations, I should be only too glad to see a Jewish force formed; it will have to be done some day presumably."[76]

One of the major conditions that was cited as being present at this time by the GOC, Police Inspector General and the HC, in consultation with political advisers and one another, was that "there is sufficient armed force at our disposal to deal with any internal situation which is reasonably likely to eventuate ... ". The statement continued "From the Government point of view, therefore, there is no need on practical grounds for a Jewish military unit unless it could be used in substitution for an equivalent number of British soldiers who could thus be released for service elsewhere."[77] The conditions would change, however, as 1938 witnessed the Arab Rebellion reach its height. Some of the personnel holding these key positions upon which the recommendations were made for the formulation of policy would also change. The momentum of the policy would remain, though, in the form of political sensitivities to the use of Jewish Forces for offensive operations.[78] Another flurry of discussions on this policy would erupt later that summer, and this would be due in no small part to Wingate.

The Mobile Column and Village Occupation

March and April of 1938 were noted for the refined British Military techniques in the tactical and operational employment of "mobile" or "flying" columns.[79] These consisted of about 100 soldiers and officers organized into two platoons, a headquarters section, a mortar detachment and a rear guard using 13 motorized transport vehicles (two of which were "Donkvans" for transporting about 10 donkeys to be used as pack animals when traveling cross-country). Weaponry consisted of rifles (.303 caliber) for most soldiers (pistols were used by soldiers with specialist duties), two "Lewis guns" (.303-caliber machine guns with 47- or 97-round drum magazines), grenades, and one mortar (3 inch).[80] These usually operated in a coordinated effort of multiple columns in order to provide a system of cordon, search, maneuver, and strike capabilities. A system of mounted battle drills was developed, and wireless transmitters were carried for coordination with each other and with aircraft that were capable of providing close air support with machine guns and bombs.[81]

The mobile columns proved effective in their engagements with large rebel bands resulting in the bands' dispersal into smaller groups. In the *History of the Disturbances in Palestine, 1936-1939*, the War Office notes that this success was followed by "A period ... when mobile columns were searching areas in an attempt to exterminate the leaders and cadres which remained with them. This proved a fruitless task. The numbers were so small, the country so difficult, and intelligence so meager that large numbers of troops were being used for exceedingly small results."[82]

After the GOC changed from Wavell to Lieutenant General Haining in April of 1938, the military assessment for the following two months was that "From our point of view the whole situation had changed radically. There were no more big military targets. At the same time the villages in the hills were being effectively terrorized and made to produce men, money and weapons."[83]

At this stage of the rebellion, the military identified that a primary component of the security solution was to separate the elusive rebels from the population through denial of the villages to the gangs. The police were acknowledged as being "stretched to the limits of their capacity," so the military expanded its village occupation scheme.[84] The results were palpable in the areas where these operations were concentrated. The now-smaller rebel gangs, however, simply moved to the fringes of the zones of occupation and changed their tactics to once again avoid decisive engagements while focusing on sabotage of infrastructure, sniping, and selective ambushes.[85]

The security situation would be noted as entering into a steady decline due to a combination of factors. The Arab population was increasingly harboring antigovernment sentiment due to their belief that partition was imminent.[86] The difficulty experienced by HM forces in bringing the rebel bands to battle left the rebels with the tactical initiative, especially as they grew in proficiency at using guerrilla tactics while acting as small bands. The rebels benefited from a constant flow of intelligence from a willing or coerced population that often resulted in the loss of operational initiative for the security forces. The rebels also maintained a largely unchecked ability to maintain logistical resupply from either compliant or terrorized and unprotected portions of the population, as well from across the frontiers by foreign sources of supply.[87]

Wingate's Intelligence Duties

Wingate's official duties as an intelligence officer from his entrance into theater and throughout this period had included coordination of the collection of information on enemy and indigenous political activity, to include participation in its collation and distribution.[88] He conducted intelligence training for other officers,[89] and he used his Arabic language skill to collect human intelligence as well as to read, file, and report information from written sources of information.[90] Wingate would steadily gain the confidence of his superiors to begin undertaking a series of special missions.

After securing permission from Wavell, Wingate carried out a reconnaissance in late March and early April 1938 in order to identify alleged smuggling routes. Fording sites along the Jordan River were presumed to be chokepoints for such activities, but an earlier reconnaissance from another party had failed to produce any information of value.[91] At some point during this period, Wingate used his Jewish contacts within the *Hagana* intelligence to secure their cooperation. This is the first recorded such cooperation that would henceforward continue to benefit Wingate.[92] He used a Jewish settlement as his base of operations, and he operated covertly (undercover as a journalist while his true identity was known only to the settlement leader). Wingate's stated intentions were first to judge the veracity of the reports about smugglers. He also intended to learn of their methods, assess the efficacy of the security forces' preventive measures, devise more effective measures, and finally to obtain specific intelligence of a smuggling operation on which he could test new concepts to counter these activities. While the mission can only be partly known to have succeeded in meeting his initial objectives because the source documents that capture this information do not survive in whole, he learned some valuable lessons. He concluded that antismuggling operations would require a battalion-sized element if the employment of forces used the current methods while acting on the typical information available in existing intelligence reports. He suggested guidelines for a new reporting format that highlighted the specificity required of intelligence reports to be "actionable." A discovery that proved to be of significance to his later counterguerrilla operations was that it was possible to operate clandestinely from Jewish settlements. This, he argued, could help prevent military operations from becoming known among the Arab population and therefore among the rebels.[93]

In May, Wingate had an opportunity to voice his opinions on the overarching politics and policy of Britain towards Palestine due to the presence of another Royal Commission that had arrived on a fact-finding trip. Based on the first Royal Commission's recommendation for partition, this second Royal Commission was sent under the leadership of Sir John

Woodhead in order to investigate the practical application of the first commission's partition plan.[94] After being introduced to the commission by Haining, Wingate was able to present his views during his session of investigative questioning by the Commission that British support of a Jewish state with a standing army was in the empire's best interests.[95]

In late May, Wingate produced a memorandum that appraised the organization and responsibilities of officers within the newly announced regional Intelligence Centers.[96] These centers were designed for the purpose of fusing information from all available government agencies (indicated as civil, police and military) for analysis and timely distribution of intelligence. The two brigades were directed to man one such center each with their brigade intelligence officers. They were to work with permanently posted representatives of the Police Force while the civil representative would liaise on a nonpermanent basis. This latter aspect of the arrangement was clearly to the chagrin of the military who desired the organizational structure to support complete and efficient cooperation from all agencies. The 14th Infantry Brigade was directed to establish one such center, while the 16th Infantry Brigade was to establish two. One of these centers was to be directed by Wingate who would be lent from the Force Headquarters Intelligence section.[97] While Wingate's memorandum titled an "appreciation on intelligence duties" has not survived, a letter from Wing Commander A.P. Ritchie (head of the Intelligence section) to Wingate confirms that he (Ritchie) and the GOC carefully considered at least one measure that Wingate proposed. Though the recommendation was thought to be unfeasible at the time due to less than "open" inter-agency relations, it is clear that Wingate recommended that the organization of the Intelligence Center include an "inspecting Intelligence officer." This was presumably to be a Military Intelligence officer that had the authority to "inspect" and therefore enforce cooperation from the other contributing agencies.[98]

Summer to Fall 1938
A Tactical Dilemma of Strategic Importance

Haining observed the effects of the military successes during the spring in breaking up the larger rebel bands in the north, then he witnessed the constant harassment caused by the smaller and elusive bands. He desired to continue effective offensive action against the rebel bands but both tactical challenges and a shortage of forces prevented further success. The bands were operating rather freely in the hills, conducting both sabotage of infrastructure as well as sniping and ambushing of HM Forces, all of which was occurring primarily at night. Before Haining was to make a personal tour of this area in July to assess the situation, measures were already being taken to counter the change in the guerrilla bands' organization and tactics.[99] Wingate had proposed a solution to Evetts for the implementation of a countergang scheme that assumed risks that were assessed as too high, due to the fact they were to be conducted by small units and at night. Wingate emphasized the practical aspects of military economy of force in conjunction with a strong argument that the risks incurred could be mitigated. He won Evetts' approval in late May and received the authorization to initiate a proof-of-concept with three British squads that would operate in conjunction with police. Wingate's proposal assessed the primary weaknesses of the military that prevented their tactical success as a lack of (1) night focused tactics and training; (2) intelligence; and (3) local knowledge of the terrain, Arabs, and Arabic. Wingate assessed the different elements within the security forces' infrastructure that could rectify the latter deficits, and he argued for the advantages of using Jewish supernumeraries on practical grounds.[100] Haining's approval would follow a few weeks later after the preliminary training and missions validated the organizational and tactical merits of Wingate's proposal.[101]

The overarching tactical dilemma for HM Forces throughout the Arab Rebellion was well understood: "In this type of guerrilla warfare ... the greatest difficulty of all is to find the enemy and bring him to action."[102] This was consistently identified as a function of the rebels' strength and HM Forces' weakness in (1) abilities to gain intelligence on the opponent; (2) maintaining their own operational security; (3) achieving surprise and maintaining the initiative; (4) knowledge of the local terrain and language; and (5) fighting at night. HM Forces were recognized as holding the advantages in military discipline as well as in firepower, but the rebels consistently mitigated these advantages. The rebels achieved this through (1) choosing to operate in small units; (2) operating at night or with the approach of nightfall; and (3) avoiding decisive engagements. As a result of HM Forces not being able to consistently maintain a sufficient troop to task ratio to dominate the entirety of their AO with the available repertoire of methods recognized as being effective, they could not (1) secure everything that required it at all times; (2) consistently and effectively use their firepower (including airpower); and (3) maneuver their relatively large forces to "close with and destroy" the enemy.[103] The prevailing military methods for employing its forces and force were proving insufficient in providing answers to the security problem that revolved around a tactical dilemma.

An Organizational and Tactical Solution to the Military Problem

Wingate's proposed solution to this tactical dilemma first appears in his "Appreciation ... of the possibilities of night movements ... with the object of putting an end to terrorism. ..."[104] He addresses the major issues of the tactical dilemma and offers innovative solutions. A new organization with an accompanying set of tactics was proposed. While even the "lessons learned" of the 1936 portion of the rebellion had identified many of these challenges, considering them as lessons learned obscures an inescapable fact: The difficulties they presented still remained to be overcome through both devising solutions and then applying them. Wingate's proposal listed as its Object: "To set up a system and undetected movement of troops and police by night, across country and into villages, surprising gangs, restoring confidence to peasants, and gaining government control of rural areas."[105] Wingate would produce a series of consecutive documents that built upon his initial proposal in order to flesh out details, add the insight gained from experimentation, and establish the organizational and tactical principles to be employed.[106]

A comparative analysis of the trends of the conventional military approach in its organization and tactics, versus those proposed by Wingate, highlights the major differences. First, the internal security strategy pursued thus far by military and police forces focused primarily on:

1. The security of the population through physical presence;

2. The physical destruction of militant rebels; and

3. The denial of the physical resources for continued rebellion (i.e. weapons and ammunition).

The means employed to achieve these goals were (corresponding to the above):

1. Police outposts, military movements to "show the flag" and village occupation by military forces;

2. The use of police and military "columns" to locate and destroy rebel bands; and

3. Patrols and obstacles along the frontiers in conjunction with village searches to block and confiscate contraband.

The noted deficiencies were (applicable to all of the above):

1. The lack of a sustainable ratio of available forces to physical security needs;

2. The lack of intelligence on rebels to include cooperation from the population in providing information;

3. A resigned attitude in continual admission that the rebels owned the tactical advantage at night; and

4. The lack of ability to achieve tactical surprise and maintain operational initiative against rebel bands in the military's effort to destroy them.

Given the military's consistent identification of the rebel bands as the primary military problem, this last point was particularly frustrating for HM Forces.[107]

Wingate's proposal of the organization and tactics that would be embodied by the Special Night Squads (SNS) would meet the noted deficiencies head on. By employing the largely untapped segment of the population in Jewish manpower available for security duties, the shortage of security forces could be addressed. This indigenous portion of the population would bring knowledge of the local terrain and language to the organization that in turn were also crucial to both knowledge of the terrain in tactical employment and language skills for intelligence collection. The lack of intelligence was to be solved initially through Wingate's own unique resources and capabilities to include his connection with the Intelligence Center and the *Hagana*, his own Arab sources of information, and his method of "forecasting" based on analysis of the enemy and terrain. The perception of the rebels' tactical advantages at night was refuted in full by Wingate. He argued that the right combination of small-unit organization, battle drills, and the discipline embodied by soldiers in conjunction with well-trained police could overcome any of the assessed tactical advantages of the rebels outright. Tactical surprise was to be gained and maintained through intelligence driven operations that employed stealth, deception, and coordinated movements of small dismounted forces. Upon making contact with the rebels, the patrols would use pre-planned battle drills to aggressively attack with "bayonet and bomb."[108]

Wingate's emphasis was not primarily on the physical destruction of the enemy, though this was intended to occur. Rather, the psychological effects of continuous small-scale but overwhelming tactical defeats through engagements at night would deter the rebels' willingness to accept the risks of mustering to conduct subversive operations. This could now occur regardless of whether the rebels were operating in large or small bands. Concerning the population, Wingate's emphasis was not primarily on their physical protection, such as that achieved through physical presence, but on a psychological state of government-enforced security, reinforced by random and unexpected visits. These visits were to be made effectual by virtue of two factors. First, surprise was expected to lead to either (1) successful searches for contraband because the rebels or rebel supporters would not have time to properly hide it; or (2) irrelevant searches because the rebels or rebel supporters' fear of the surprise visits outweighed the risk that they were willing to accept in order to retain contraband. Second, the tactical dominance that the unit represented over the rebels, and therefore the rebels' ability to terrorize the population, would lead to cooperation of the population with the government. This would in turn lead to the population supplying the government with information on the rebels, which would further result in more effective targeting of rebel bands.[109] Operational initiative and momentum was to be maintained by steady expansion of the organization and methods until guerrilla activities were neutralized, after which police or police auxiliaries that were trained in the new methods could be employed to maintain security for governmental control of the area.

The Special Night Squads

Wingate's establishment of the SNS organization was clearly intended both by Wingate and the 16th Infantry Brigade (in whose battle-space his Intelligence Center was operating) to serve two primary functions. The first function was to operate as a night-time battle-space owner in which the organization would conduct "moving ambushes." These were intended to neutralize guerrilla activities and build public confidence in the efficacy of the government security forces to maintain security. The purpose of this function was ultimately for the "gaining [of] Government control of rural areas."[110] The secondary function was for the organization to act as a test bed for both small-unit night-time offensive tactics, as well as for an organization composed of both British Officers and Soldiers as well as police. Effective tactics and tactical training, once refined, were to be synthesized, published, and disseminated along with a reproducible training plan suitable for both expanding the organization as well as distributing the capabilities across the force.[111] The SNS was associated with the Brigade Intelligence Center and comprised its action arm. Wingate was afforded all the latitudes and authorities for direction and employment of the SNS as would be expected of a commander of a conventional unit, but he reported directly to the brigade commander.

The SNS as an organization was composed of three "squads" under the overall command of Wingate. Three British Officers acted as Squad leaders, each leading 24 to 36 Jewish supernumeraries that worked in conjunction with 10 to 12 British Soldiers. The soldiers trained the supernumeraries and then operated with them for tactical employment, but the soldiers themselves were not permanently attached to the SNS and therefore would rotate back to their unit to be replaced by others. The SNS use of the term Squad was, therefore, an organizational term for the composition of forces stated above as distinguished from a typical British squad that would normally consist of 8 to 12 personnel. The operational unit strength of the SNS organization as a whole at any given time generally consisted of about 100 to 150 personnel, though many more Jewish supernumeraries were trained. Many of these supernumeraries would operate continuously throughout the lifespan of the SNS and therefore become the veteran experts in employing their tactics. Others would often rotate in and out of operational status. The use of the term Squad, therefore, was either an intentional misnomer in order to mislead others as to its actual size, or it was meant to be understood in a more general sense as representative of a tactical formation without reference to its actual size at all. The SNS would sometimes vary the size of formations employed on individual operations in order to meet its specific requirements, yet each such operational element was also referred to as a Squad when acting in this capacity regardless of size. Wingate himself would assume tactical leadership of a Squad as well as operational command of multiple squads acting in conjunction with each other. Wingate's initial recommendation for the name of the organization was Night Movement Group, though this would be changed to SNS before operations commenced.[112]

Evetts was intent on destroying the rebel bands and had desired the tactical capabilities within his force to use surprise and the maintenance of the initiative to achieve this effect.[113] He distinctly realized, first, that this would require owning the night, and second, that the current skill sets and techniques for such night actions were not up to par within the force.[114] Evetts, therefore, determined that the capability would have to be developed from the bottom up. The language of Wingate's proposal points to Evetts' influence in the broader sense of the understanding of the tactical problem and the available traditional military solutions. Wingate's proposal, however, appears to be a unique synthesis of his own:

1. Military experience.

2. Understanding of the operational environment.

3. Views on the risk assessment and its possible mitigation.

4. Capacities as an intelligence officer.

5. Personal influence among the Jewish population and its leadership.

6. Overarching strategic objectives of forming the nucleus of a Jewish Army for protection of British interests in the region.

Evetts would vigorously resource and support Wingate's proposal.[115] Within a month of the inception of the SNS, it had begun to produce tangible military results, and Evetts took note. During the first week of July, Evetts published an operations instruction complete with a set of control measures specifically for night ambushes and "night work" for the security forces operating within his brigade's AO. Night ambushes were to be conducted at the discretion of both battalion commanders and supernumerary police units within separate and defined areas of responsibility. Night Work was charged as the responsibility of battalion commanders in conjunction with the police authorities throughout all remaining areas of their AO. The SNS was allotted its own AO for Night Work.[116] The operations instruction's association between night ambushes being conducted around static posts implies, in operational terms, the concept of active versus passive defense. The delineation between night ambush and Night Work is intentionally nuanced, with the latter assuming an even more aggressive style of operations. At the tactical level it was offensive, though at the operational level it could be argued to be offensive or defensive, depending on the operational context in which it was framed.

The SNS operations were considered Night Work and are known to include "moving ambushes" or movements to contact. These were coordinated movements of small units that actively sought visual or physical contact with rebels from which an assault battle drill could be employed to achieve a decisive tactical engagement.[117] Other types of operations conducted at night, in distinction from night ambushes and otherwise common nighttime activities such as mounted patrols of roads, are known to include infiltration and pre-positioning of cordons for village searches that would commence at dawn.[118] The Jewish supernumerary police were not officially addressed as being given Night Work responsibilities apart from their participation in the SNS. The use of Jewish security personnel for offensive operations had already caused friction with civil authorities due to the SNS in mid-June. The local District Commissioner, who had political jurisdiction over the SNS AO, ordered Wingate to cancel an operation precisely on this account. Wingate forwarded the written prohibition to Evetts alongside his intelligence-driven plan to interdict an expected sabotage operation directed at the wire fence along the northern frontier. The intelligence proved correct as the saboteurs struck at the time and place indicated, which was also duly noted in Wingate's correspondence, and the prohibition was removed.[119]

The tactical successes of the SNS under Wingate's command had produced significant results relative to its small size and minimal resources from June until Wingate's departure on leave in mid-October. As the experience of the force grew, and Wingate's confidence in them, the consistent practice of small dismounted patrols conducting movements to contact expanded to include coordinated operations using most or all of the available Squads. These larger operations included the use of multiple dispersed infiltration routes that either (1) provided mutually supporting columns employed on search and destroy missions, or (2) converged for the envelopment of rebel gangs that were occupying villages or supposed safe-sites. This latter type of SNS operation often employed techniques to either dislodge or lure the rebel gang out of the village. An area ambush would be preplanned along potential rebel egress routes so that one or more engagements would likely be successful from the series of static ambushes. The initiation of contact from such an ambush Squad would then provide a trigger for the others to displace and reposition or conduct movements to contact.[120]

The friction of battle sometimes blurred the distinction between the type of SNS operation that was planned and the one that would eventually be executed due to unforeseen developments in the situation. One example of such a mission took place on the night of 11-12 July centering on an area that included the villages of Ein Mahil and Dabburiya. Intelligence indicated that a rebel gang that had recently occupied villages and attacked police stations was overnighting in the area. Wingate narrowed down the potential enemy locations through pattern analysis in conjunction with physical and map reconnaissance. The location of a police station in Dabburiya led Wingate to believe that the village of Ein Mahil was the more likely enemy location, so he devised an operation employing 32 British

Soldiers and 55 Jewish supernumeraries. The plan was to flush the rebel gang out of the village and into a series of ambushes laid by supporting SNS along the most likely enemy egress route that happened to lead towards Dabburiyah. The squad closest to Dabburiyah ended up making contact with the enemy first, so the squads displaced and converged on the sound of the guns. Nine rebels were confirmed Killed in Action (KIA) through recovery of their bodies, though 15 were estimated to be KIA along with 20 wounded in action. The rebel leader fled the engagement early and, due to the casualties inflicted upon the rebel gang, they would not conduct operations for another seven weeks. The SNS suffered one Jewish supernumerary KIA and a few wounded in action overall, including Wingate,[121] who would be awarded the Distinguished Service Order after this action. This was a particularly exceptional and rare event because he was junior officer and it was technically "peacetime."

The patrols conducted by the SNS were often long and arduous endeavors. One that took place in August was recorded as covering 25 miles, and this not only occurred in the mountainous region north of Tiberius but it included an engagement that killed four rebels. The latter half of August was spent in experimentation by the SNS for operating in conjunction with an infantry regiment, but Wingate would conclude that "large combinations in this guerrilla fighting defeat their own object. This is a subaltern's war."[122] The noteworthy events in September included an authorized expansion of training Jewish supernumeraries[123] as well as an action at Khirbet Beit Lidd that rendered 14 rebels KIA as proved by recovery of their bodies and included a prominent rebel *sheikh*.[124] Haining would again praise the SNS in an official dispatch for this operation.[125] Information gathered during this action led to subsequent intelligence-driven operations to include one against a mayor who was implicated by documents found on the rebel leader.[126]

A set of SNS operations conducted 3 and 4 October proved some of the most notable, not only because of what they were able to achieve but because of what the other security forces could not. A rebel infiltration of Tiberius resulted in the massacre of 19 Jewish civilians. Garrisons of military and police were unable to pursue the rebel gang, but SNS forces that were operating west of Tiberius intercepted the rebel element as it departed. Six enemy casualties were confirmed KIA through recovery of their bodies while "at least forty casualties must have been suffered by the enemy".[127] The next morning, Wingate was traveling alone to Nazareth, presumably to the Intelligence Center, when he spotted two rebel leaders in taxis that were also possible participants or facilitators in the previous night's rebel actions. Wingate conducted a link-up with nearby SNS (less than 20 personnel) and pursued the rebel leader. An engagement ensued at the summit of Mount Tabor and, despite their numerical inferiority and hasty attack, they killed the rebel leader and an estimated 13 more rebels.[128]

Wingate's summary of achievements for the SNS from June to October 1938 included more than 70 rebel KIA confirmed through body recovery, with the estimate that "at least double this number were killed, and as many as 300 wounded." Wingate himself compiled this summary, but he did so in a letter to Evetts. The information he was giving was immediately verifiable, and certainly intended for an audience well beyond Evetts himself. It is likely that Wingate's purpose in summarizing the exploits of the SNS was to silence critics, and to do so with Evetts' authority behind the verification of the details. Wingate closes his summary with the claim that "I do not think that there is a battalion, let alone a company, in Palestine, that can show such a record, even for a whole tour of duty."[129]

Evetts' long-term intentions in underwriting the tactical experimentation of the SNS were two-fold. First, he recognized their tactical value for countering the rebel bands and for enhancing force-wide capabilities. Second, he saw their potential operational value for a sustainable economy-of-force mission in securing rural areas. These intentions are evidenced, first, by the procedure with which Wingate was required to report. This included submission of operational after-action reports that served not only the function of typical reporting requirements but also as validation of the proof-of-concept. These reports included the submission of tactical "lessons learned" and training plans as well.[130] Second, Wingate was certainly under the impression that his communications with Evetts implied the intention to expand both his newly formulated tactics force-wide and the SNS itself as an independent tactical formation of British and Jewish character. In Wingate's proposal that he submitted to Evetts for the establishment of the SNS, he states that "As lessons are learned and experience gained, the Group can be expanded both with troops and with supernumeraries. The ultimate goal is continual movement by night of ambush squads in all areas. ... "[131] This initial expectation for the expansion of the SNS would be followed up with a limited request for expansion within five weeks of its inception. Another specific request for expansion was initiated in September, but this time it was larger in scale and in accord with his initial expectation to be able to do so after about three months.[132] Evetts would at this time recommend the duplication of the SNS organization and tactics for use by all three brigades. Amid higher-level discussions for the potential disbandment of the SNS, Evetts wrote to the higher headquarters that "I think it would be a great mistake to break up this organization and I consider it should be used for all three [Brigades]. Capt. Wingate has asked my permission to write privately to the GOC on the question of training and expanding SNS and 'Police' for the whole country and ... I have given this permission."[133]

Haining states in his official report on operations during this period that "One of my objectives has always been that we should be 'top-dog' by Night as well as by day. Consequently great efforts have been made by all units to re-establish Night control of the country by constant patrols, ambushes and searches. ... I cannot speak too highly of ... the special Night Squads that have been organized ... for active offensive Night work."[134] After Haining's declaration of widespread emphasis and effort on night operations during this period, the successes of the SNS were put into the broader context of the tactical dilemma by the same report. Haining states that "effective and widespread control of the country by Night is a most difficult problem. The advantage must be with the lawless and the saboteur, and the forces of law and order suffer from numerous disadvantages by comparison."[135] Wingate's submittal of his proposal for the SNS in June declares that this focus on night operations had not yet taken place prior to this time, so it is unclear whether Wingate influenced Haining's emphasis on night operations or if Wingate's proposal merely coincided with the shift. Wingate heartily disagreed with the assessment of strengths and weaknesses favoring the rebels at night, and he disagreed with any account that HM Forces' were displaying a zeal for night operations. In the proposal, he criticized the police and military for not conducting operations at night "as a general rule" and he also commented on the ineffectiveness of their procedures for engaging the enemy at night.[136]

Haining praises Wingate by name in his continuation of the report. He also mentions the use of Jewish supernumeraries operating within the SNS as well, albeit specifically in relation to "protecting the I.P.C. [Iraq Petroleum Company] pipeline".[137] The SNS operated from three separate settlements. Initially, the squads were operating primarily along the pipeline; however, only one of them would be habitually concentrated on engaging the rebel gangs conducting sabotage of the pipeline.[138] Wingate would later recount that "The prevention of pipe-line sabotage is, properly speaking, the task of only twenty four of the Jewish SNS. Nearly all the SNS operations of importance took place elsewhere and for different objects [purposes of missions]."[139] Here, "twenty four of the Jewish SNS" is a reference to Jewish supernumeraries that would make up part of one Squad within the three-Squad structure of the SNS as an organization.

Wingate's intention in the beginning was to operate near the pipeline, but this was not primarily for its protection. This was not only generally an area of heavy activity for rebel bands, but the rebels' targeting of the pipeline for sabotage simply increased the chances of the SNS for making contact with the rebels as they approached or departed from their target. The bottlenecks along infiltration routes and the lure of wire fence along the northern frontier for rebel sabotage also offered similar circumstances that focused Wingate's employment of the SNS.[140] Wingate's later defense of the efficacy of the SNS organization and the techniques that they employed against rebel gangs would require him to point out that pipeline security was never the priority mission. It would, however, reasonably appear to be so from the point of view of anyone who was not aware of the operations first hand but had only read about them from the official military reports.[141]

The emphasis in the official reports concerning the use of the SNS for pipeline protection appears to be an attempt by Haining to achieve two results. Haining's first objective appears to be to exploit a loophole in the policy of non-use of Jews for offensive operations off of their own land. The history of the security forces employed for infrastructure protection in Palestine had well-established roots for being composed of units of largely Jewish character.[142] There was even a Jewish-proposed security scheme before the employment of the SNS for 200 Jewish *ghaffirs* (security guards) to guard the pipeline. This constituted yet another attempt to exploit the momentum already in place for this duty being recognized as one suitable for a security force of Jewish character. This scheme was either picked up by Wingate or similarly developed by him to exploit the same momentum. It was Wingate's intention to train a suitable force of locally based Jewish supernumeraries that could then replace the SNS in the area for continued pipeline protection operations while the SNS focused elsewhere.[143]

The second objective of Haining appears to be to test the waters in challenging the policy and influencing its change, albeit this would eventually prove to be limited in scope when compared to Wingate's intentions. Haining's official reports were not only circulated among the War Office but in the Colonial Office as well. Haining's official reports and dispatches on operations were one way in which he, as GOC Palestine, fulfilled not only his duty to inform but to "advise" the policy-makers on the effects of their policy. The nature of "advising" in this manner allowed for arguments to be made based primarily on pragmatism while generally void of politicized emotion. It was certainly expected, however, that robust and highly politicized discussions would be generated among the policy-makers. Haining's reports entailed an element of taking action based on what was deemed as military necessity, and then waiting for the lag time of political discussion to unfold while a stronger case was potentially being built to counter, if need be, being told to stop what he was doing. Haining had consulted with the HC over the SNS and they were both in agreement to support the organization and its controversial use of force by Jewish supernumeraries before asking for permission. The HC's letter to the Secretary of State for the Colonies clearly expresses support for the overall policy in place, though he carefully notes his reasoning for suitable small-scale departures. He further confirms that these decisions were arrived at in consultation with the GOC. He states "that the broad principle of employing armed Jews for defensive purposes only and in areas mainly Jewish has been adhered to, although a certain latitude in the application of that principle has been necessitated by varying circumstances. I should like … to emphasize that in every case the modifications have been dictated by reasons of utilitarian expediency and not at all by political

... considerations ... [and that I might] have to extend the employment of armed Jewish supernumeraries in cases where the local circumstances demand it."[144] The parallel reporting on the SNS by both Haining and the HC proved to stir up inquiry from "higher" as expected. The Secretary of State for the Colonies wrote to the HC in August, "I note that a small column of Jews and British troops is being employed on operations in Galilee, including (on occasion) 'ambush work'. I assume that 'ambush work' can properly be regarded as falling within the category of defensive or protective operations[?]"[145]

The general policy of disallowing security forces of largely Jewish character to conduct offensive operations outside of Jewish areas was again confirmed through interdepartmental meetings as a result of the reintroduction of the subject by the GOC and HC's reporting. The Colonial Office condoned the limited departure from this policy with regard to the employment of the SNS based on the GOC and HC's support of the unit and its operations. The understanding appears to be that the SNS was not to significantly exceed the known extent of its initial composition except for practical expediency, and that the details would be reported. The political considerations, as discussed, included what were anticipated as the negative effects of a policy reversal both on the greater Arab and Muslim worlds, as well as on the Arab elements of the security forces in Palestine. These concerns were repeatedly considered well-founded within both the military and political spheres. Palestine's internal security concerns, despite reaching their height in 1938, would consistently fall short of the advantage to disadvantage analysis for a wholesale policy reversal.[146] The red-lines for a policy reversal that would allow massive expansion of the use of Jews within the security forces were well discussed and articulated. These included, first, the possibility of an "insurrection following the publication of the Partition Commission's [second Royal Commission] report" in which both the Jewish and Arab populations would be involved, and second, the outbreak of major conflict in the anticipated war among European powers for which the military would have to transfer forces out of Palestine.[147]

Haining's testing of the policy was for limited objectives in the end, namely, to preserve the SNS as it was initially organized and employed in the heart of the rebel gang activity. It is unclear if this was a change from earlier and more overarching desires for a policy change that would allow the military to expand the organizational and operational concepts utilized by the SNS. Such a development would have elevated Wingate's organizational and tactical "experiment" to a centerpiece of the overall internal security strategy. Such a desire by Haining, if it existed, could have been mitigated during the course of deliberations with the HC and other governmental departments. By September, Haining would frame his desires for achieving efficiency in his employment of the military in terms of economy of force. He wanted to achieve localized security objectives while freeing the military from duties that could effectively be accomplished by other units within the security forces infrastructure. The SNS experiment was but one authorization among many concurrent plans that were in conflict with strict adherence to the policy. He "recommended the enlistment of a number of temporary police (Jewish) for service with the army."[148] Haining had communicated that such duties would include convoy protection as well as infrastructure repair and protection, but it is unclear as to the extent that he might have intended to expand the SNS within this framework of Jewish security forces. It is also unclear whether these requests were intended to obscure an attempt at limited expansion.[149]

The War Office published a document in 1939 that chronicled "The Development of the Palestine Police Force. ... " The SNS and the police attached to the military, as requested by Haining and referenced above, are noted to have resulted from the "shortage of troops. ... " It is further noted that "In the case of the Special Night Squads organization, the enrolment of a limited number of Jews was agreed to by the Secretary of State on the understanding that they would be used on offensive-defensive tasks under the direct command of and together with British troops, (e.g. protection of IRAQ Oil pipe line). Although the hybrid nature of these categories has caused considerable administrative difficulties, they have fulfilled their tasks satisfactorily, especially the men of the Special Night Squads."[150] The military and political situation, however, was about to change. These changes would increase the amount of forces available to Haining, and they would therefore affect his employment of those forces. These changes would also advance the heightened political sensitivity towards the use of the Jews within the security forces.

No matter what Haining's initial goals were or how much he might have desired to provide cover for the expansion of the SNS as an organization, the stabilization of the SNS strength that did occur was in conflict with Wingate's goals and expectations. Wingate desired an overarching policy change that would lead to permanent and expanding formation of units of British and Jewish character within the security forces apparatus in Palestine. In turn, he hoped that these would form the nucleus of a Jewish Army that was in keeping with his own strategic assessment for Palestine's role in securing British interests in the region.[151] The policy constraints on the employment of force for security forces of Jewish character was not one that Wingate had to confront directly. Wingate had secured the "stretching" of that policy through military channels as represented by the authorization and resourcing of the SNS. The SNS made good on Wingate's promises, but his hopes for expansion of the SNS organization and tactics had been blunted by the policy. This policy conflict would prove to be the fulcrum for the limitations that would prevent the organizational and operational expansion of his military "solution" to the security problem.

Having expended his options and his patience, Wingate was left to assess what course of action that he should pursue.

Pivot Point

The Munich Agreement, which occurred in late September of 1938, ceded the Sudetenland (parts of then Czechoslovakia) to Germany. British tensions over the rising Nazi threat remained, but the pressure for maintenance of a military force capable of immediate response to their military threat had eased some in the wake of this event. Some believed that Hitler had limited aims that had been sufficiently satisfied with the terms, while most would at least concede that the seemingly unavoidable war was at any rate postponed for the near term. British troops were now available, and they were needed. In Palestine, the security situation had deteriorated to its worst yet in September and October. The nearly complete loss of control by the civil government led to military control, but the now steady flow of reinforcements that would amount to a second division required time to arrive and prepare for operations.[152] Entire sections of Jerusalem fell under rebel control and were not able to be retaken until the end of October. The Palestine Police were put under the operational control of the military, but the Arab element was disarmed due to its unreliability and ineffectiveness.[153] Two able division commanders, however, would join the fight: Generals Ryan Neith O'Connor and Bernard Montgomery.

In October, international politics and its impact on the policy in Palestine were again being reassessed. In Cairo, a meeting by the World Inter-parliamentary Congress of Arab and Moslem Countries for the Defense of Palestine accentuated British fears concerning the threat of Arab and Muslim countries' potential alliances with Germany and Italy.[154] In London, interdepartmental meetings between the War, Colonial, and Foreign Offices in consultation with the HC concluded that the outstanding consideration of foreign political consequence in determining domestic policy in Palestine was the safeguard of the greater Arab and Muslim worlds' goodwill towards Britain. Their assessments and conclusions for the way forward included:

1. Consideration of the situation throughout the empire in the event of future European crisis;

2. That the Balfour Declaration was a mistake;

3. That an independent Jewish state in Palestine was infeasible;

4. That British rule should continue over Jewish and Arab cantons but with their increased governmental participation; and

5. That consideration of either an Arab or Jewish state in Palestine was likely irrelevant because the whole of Palestine would eventually be absorbed into an Arab federation.

This last consideration, however, was only valid as long as Jewish immigration was sufficiently restricted to keep them in the minority. Early November witnessed the release of the Second Royal Commission's Report that declared partition as an unviable option. Simultaneously with the release of this report, a conference was proposed to discuss alternate solutions among British, Jewish, and Arab (Palestinian and non-Palestinian) officials for the way forward in Palestine.[155]

The Jewish leadership was in crisis mode as the details of the forthcoming British announcements were being discovered in October. The land allotment to the Jews that was to be proposed by the British Government as a starting point for negotiations was smaller than that of the First Royal Commission's proposal. This, in conjunction with the proposed restrictions on Jewish immigration, was deemed unacceptable by the Jewish leadership, who then began to mobilize in order to put political pressure on the British Government. Throughout the previous year, it had been increasingly difficult for the Jewish leadership to reign in the militant Jewish fringe that had increased the intensity of their reprisal attacks and flouted the policy of *havlagah*. British security forces had, however, targeted the Jewish political and military organizations that were behind such attacks and significantly degraded their ability to operate prior to this tenuous period.[156] While the policy of *havlagah* would again be commended by Haining in a secret cypher message to the Chief of the Imperial General Staff in January 1939, he would also note the period had witnessed a resurgence in the militant factions of the Jews. He adds his assessment that "any further concessions to Rebels may very likely lead, in my view, to more than protests on the part of the Jews."[157] One historian's summary of the Arab Rebellion up to this point was that "The sponsors of the Arab revolt had . . . won two major political victories by the fall of 1938."[158] These were stated as the British Government's admission "that the Palestine Mandate was unworkable" and that there was at this point a "scuttling of the partition scheme, even before any attempt was made to implement it."[159] The conclusion was that "These events taught the lesson that the use of violence as a political weapon produced results which otherwise appeared unobtainable."[160] This "political weapon" would remain an effective instrument for another year in the Arab Rebellion, but the Jewish leadership would, on the whole, decide to keep theirs holstered in favor of diplomacy due to their assessment of the greater threat to their political goals being the rise of Nazi Germany.

Wingate Speaks to Power

Wingate took leave in mid-October and left Palestine for London. He had noted earlier that summer that he intended to take leave during the winter, and it is also likely that the accumulation of mental and physical demands over the several preceding months had influenced his decision.[161] It is unclear if the decision to take leave was also driven in part by his perceived sense of "duty" to voice his opinions about policy and strategy in Palestine.[162] This would, however, be the way in which he would spend much of his time there. Some biographers suggest that requests by the Jewish leadership for his aid in engaging the policy-makers factored into his decision.[163] The British Army of the time prided itself on being apolitical, and Wingate's actions would take him well beyond "the line" considered appropriate for a military officer of his rank and official capacity.

The knowledge of Wingate's exact words and actions with many senior British political and military officials during his leave are difficult to establish with certainty. Most of the secondary sources repeat the early biographers who used personal interviews and recollections from individuals that were not always cited and are no longer verifiable. The weight of evidence among the primary sources that does exist, in conjunction with Wingate's determined persistence to influence the policy in Palestine both before and after this period, all point to his extensive engagement of both policy-makers and those influential among the policy-makers. Even if some of the unverifiable meetings were not conducted as supposed, the first-hand sources citing his political involvement are extensive enough to establish this facet of his influence on the policy towards Palestine.[164] In addition to this, Wingate's written documents throughout this period and beyond clearly state the common threads of his opinions on policy and strategy.[165]

Ben-Gurion recalls that he, Weizmann, and Wingate met with Lord Lloyd (former High Commissioner to Egypt and future Secretary of State for the Colonies) in late October. The three had proposed an alternative plan to Lloyd than those that they had known to be under consideration by the British Government for introduction at the forthcoming British-Jewish-Arab Conference in London. Wingate addressed the strategic importance of Palestine to Britain and their advantage in securing its interests there by means of an armed Jewish state.[166] A letter from the Chief of the Imperial General Staff to Lloyd confirms his receipt of Lloyd's letter, recommending that he meet with Wingate. The outcome of the proposed meeting is unknown, but the letter also indicates that Wingate had already met with the Director of Military Operations and Intelligence.[167] Wingate would contact Basil Liddell Hart (military historian, journalist, and strategist that had influence with the Secretary of State for War Leslie Hore-Belisha) and provide him with documents concerning the SNS. Liddell Hart would in turn pass along a letter of introduction and the SNS documents to Winston Churchill, but it appears that Wingate might have already met and discussed Palestine with Churchill through another channel.[168] The Wingate biographer and Middle East expert Christopher Sykes submits that Wingate even secured a meeting with the Secretary of State for the Colonies, Malcolm MacDonald.[169] The news of Wingate's activities in London reached Palestine, and because of this he would not return to the SNS but was ordered to Force Headquarters in Jerusalem upon his arrival in early December.[170]

Winter 1938 to Winter 1939
Wingate Sidelined in Palestine

Wingate's superiors sidelined him for his actions in London. The details surrounding this event invite analysis, and they are dealt with in detail in the concluding section of this case study because the source information that provides insight into this affair was compiled at the end of Wingate's tour in Palestine. The SNS continued under a younger British Officer after Wingate's removal from command. Any considerations for future expansion were dropped not only because of the reaffirmation and hardening of policy concerning the employment of Jewish security forces but because a division of reinforcements had arrived in country. The SNS operations refocused on infrastructure protection along the pipeline for three reasons. First, the rebels again shifted tactics to concentrate on sabotage of infrastructure because of the increased military pressure.[171] Second, pipeline protection remained a necessary task and there doesn't appear to have been any better solutions than the economy-of-force mission provided by constant night-time dismounted patrolling. Even with the military reinforcements in country, the other available military methods to conduct such a mission of secondary importance were not practical in terms of force requirements. Third, the assumption of risk for the larger and more expansive SNS operations was no longer acceptable either tactically or politically. Wingate would later comment on his being informed that he would no longer command the SNS as resulting from the "great changes [that] had come about. The country was full of troops and it was no longer found necessary to rely so much on the loyal section of the population. For political reasons a policy of 'passive' use of the SNS was embarked upon and pursued until they virtually ceased to exist in a recognizable form."[172]

Waning of Rebellion

Meanwhile, the changes in the operational environment and the internal security strategy in Palestine would eventually lead to the waning of the Arab Rebellion as a Big War was waxing in Europe. The division of reinforcements that arrived in the fall of 1938 enabled robust efforts to execute and enforce the military authorities that were granted under military control. This allowed for a change in strategy.[173] Haining's plan was first to re-establish security and governmental control in the major cities and across the south. Then, he would secure the lines of communication and expand operations into the rural areas in the north. Efforts to reorganize and rebuild the Palestine Police were simultaneously undertaken under military direction and control. Disarmament of the population was a major focus of operations. Haining understood that the objective would never completely be attained, but he would comment on the importance of the effort for both its practical value and its political effect. Haining stated that "it is essential that every endeavor should be made to collect as many arms as possible in order that a slackening of the rebellion consequential to the publication of the new British policy may not be looked on as a moral victory for the Arabs, and especially to reduce the possibility of armed disorders breaking out again at any later date when conditions might appear more favourable for rebel activities."[174]

The London conferences of Arab, British, and Jewish delegations in the Spring of 1939 ended in deadlock despite the British threats of unilateral decision on Palestine's future. Meanwhile, the Arab Rebellion was fracturing with some rebel factions turning against each other in either blood-feuds or attempts to stop the Arab-British cycle of violence. When the British Government released its white paper on 17 May, it was clear that the Arab demands had been given the maximum deference short of a total appearance to have ceded political ground to violence. The reception of the announcement by the Palestinian Arab community was mixed as many demands were still left unmet, but continual military pressure had exhausted a large portion of the Arab population. Sporadic terrorist attacks would continue by both Arabs and an enlarged Jewish militant fringe, but the outbreak of the European hostilities with the Nazi invasion of Poland in September sobered the resistance to the realities of worsening hardship amidst the political and economic crises that both communities were enduring. The rebellion fizzled out.[175]

Wingate's Fallout and Farewell

Wingate would remain in Jerusalem until his transfer back to the United Kingdom in May 1939.[176] His annual confidential reports (officer evaluation report) written by his rater, Wing Commander Ritchie, and his senior rater, Lieutenant General Haining, criticized him among their praise for his other exceptional qualities as an officer.[177] Haining, after praising Wingate's actions with the SNS, states his major criticism of Wingate, which are along the same lines as Ritchie's major criticism, as "[his] tendency ... to play for his own ends and likings instead of playing for the side ... has become so marked, and a matter of such general comment as to render his services in the Intelligence branch nugatory and embarrassing."[178]

Wingate would file a complaint in rebuttal of the critical comments made by Ritchie. Some sections from his lengthy statement are worthy of evaluation and consideration here. Wingate states:

> It is indeed owing to the fact that my sympathy does not waiver with every political tide that I owe my standing and my potential usefulness to His Majesty's service. It is certain that to express sympathy with Zionist aims is to court wide unpopularity in official circles. It is also widely believed and widely stated without contradiction that this is not so when pro-Arab feelings are expressed.

> No doubt the distinguished officers that read this will say that there should be no question of a political bias. I agree, I had none. My bias was and is Imperial, but I differ from Wing Commander Ritchie and most of his brother officers in my views as to what is the true Imperial interest. Unless to be in a small minority is to be wrong there is no reason to think I am so until my arguments have been answered. I know that my views are shared by some many distinguished officers and I have no doubt that in a few years they will be proved correct. In any case my free expression of them to my superiors was a duty. … I would be judged by results, not opinions. My public and private support of the Jews was obligatory. They had always been loyal to me and to Great Britain. … I became during my official studies convinced that the Imperial, Jewish, and Arab interests all ally in one direction. I have never made the slightest secret of my views form my superiors. Persons who have not served in Palestine will not readily believe the extent of the indiscretion, the violence of partisanship even in official circles.[179]

Here, Wingate's argument displays a line of logic that connects the results of his receiving critical comments in his annual confidential report by Ritchie (and likely his being withdrawn from SNS command as well) as being caused by personal differences in political opinion and assessment of British Imperial strategic interest. As strong as Wingate's argument might have been if these were the only factors, it does not appear that Wingate captures the central issue, namely, his meetings in London. Sykes quotes a letter of comment by Ritchie in which Ritchie records that he told Wingate that he "had acted improperly as an officer serving in Palestine in obtaining an interview with the Secretary of State for the Colonies."[180]

The nature of Wingate's relationship with Ritchie was likely a strained one.[181] This could have been a result of any number of factors, not least of which was Wingate's strong personality and willingness to forcefully put forth his arguments regardless of another's authority or position. Wingate would likely prove to be a difficult subordinate for almost any first line supervisor, let alone one to whom Wingate's mantra was disagreeable. Wingate states that his political and strategic opinions were communicated openly and often. There is no reason to doubt these claims, as it would have not only been in character for Wingate but refutable by Ritchie to the effect of weakening Wingate's argument. Any differences of opinion that Ritchie might have had concerning Wingate's pro-Zionist sympathies and strategic assessments, had not led to any known adverse actions towards Wingate by Ritchie prior to Wingate's activities on leave. Therefore, this raises doubts concerning the validity of Wingate's logic on the central issue behind Ritchie's (and Haining's) statements. While Ritchie does not explicitly reference Wingate's meetings with senior military and political officials in the annual confidential report, he does make a statement that captures the essence of the "line" that Wingate chose to cross. Ritchie says of Wingate that "his ardent nature which gives him the power to pursue an objective enthusiastically often obscures his judgment and obstructs his sense of proportion."

In Wingate's continuation of his rebuttal, he not only continues the aforementioned line of logic but he also continues a theme introduced in the segment of his rebuttal above. He identifies that the extent of his usefulness in service to the Crown was tied to his extreme position of support for the Jewish cause. Wingate writes,

> It is unwise to forget that during the past three years to sympathise with Arabs was to side with the rebel, to sympathise with Jews was to side with our friends. ... I early formed the theories which I was later to put into successful practice. Briefly me [sic] theory was that in order to master the rebellion it was essential to gain continual surprise. This was possible only by employing to the utmost the resources of the loyal element in the population. ... You cannot gain the confidence and loyalty of an alien community without publicly defending it and making known your sympathy for it. The value of hanging at least one officer trusted and loved by each section of the population that remains loyal is evident. I had supposed that my superiors realized this and approved my policy generally. Naturally the difficulty of filling such a role is immense and I am open to criticism. I welcome such criticism so long as my bona fides [character] are not called into question and it is realized that I must be a true friend to the Jews if I am to command their loyalties. I am not ashamed to say that I am a real and devoted admirer of the Jews and I submit with all respect the opinion that had more officers shared my views the rebellion would have come to a speedy conclusion some years ago. ... [By] creating and maintaining this connection I performed an important service to the Crown. ... I further claim that future developments are likely to render my services in Palestine as again of great use and that they should be employed there.[182]

First, Wingate's opinion that using the Jews in countering the Arab Rebellion would have led to a relatively quick achievement of military success was not a unique point of view. In the War Office's publication *Military Lessons of the Arab Rebellion, 1936*, it states:

> The Civil Service and the armed forces of the country had been built up upon Arabs, and there were not sufficient trained Jews to replace them. In the end, force of circumstances compelled the Government to organize the Jews in the defence of law and order, and in particular a large force of Supernumerary Police was raised. But by then it was too late to provide in full the organization and training necessary with a result that their real value was never properly exploded [exploited]. There is little doubt that in the end the authorities benefited by the subterranean defence organizations which their policy had forced underground, and it might perhaps have been better to have legalized and controlled at an earlier period the very natural activities which developed below the surface.[183]

This view has easily identifiable merits, but if it ignores the political implications in Palestine and the strategic implications for the greater empire, then it is also over-simplistic. The statement in the *Military Lessons...* assumes the feasibility of employing indigenous security forces composed of separate elements of distinctly Arab or Jewish character simultaneously on a large scale. The policy-makers, whose responsibility it was to consider the political and strategic ramifications of such a choice, never deemed this course of action acceptable. While the Jewish supernumeraries would be employed as an adjunct to the Palestine Police that was composed primarily of Arabs, this would be justified on grounds of practical necessity for localized security needs and on a relatively small scale. It was never done on political grounds or as a function of overarching policy.

Wingate's comments, however, don't advocate such a middle road of employing indigenous security forces made up of units distinctly composed of each segment of the population. His comments point to the future possibility of British Forces operating solely with an indigenous security force of Jewish character. His thoughts were developing on this issue throughout this period and beyond for securing British interests in Palestine and the region, but they consistently advocated a Jewish state with a standing army as being fundamental to securing British interests. The strategic thought and argument surrounding Palestine and the British Empire that Wingate espoused before, during and after this letter of complaint had their merits. However, once again, the difference in opinion between Wingate and his superiors is not the crux of the issue, but it was his unprofessionalism in going outside of the approved channels that ultimately resulted in a loss of trust in Wingate's ability to submit his own opinions to established policy.

Wingate's own defense highlights that his greatest potential for service to the Crown in Palestine was inextricably linked to his support of, affiliation with, and built trust among the Jews and their leadership. This is most certainly true, but the realization of this potential was in turn linked to whether or not the overarching policy would allow this relationship to be exploited to its fullest (in Wingate's point of view). The development of the British Government's thought and practice of the policy pursued towards Palestine has already been established in this study. The political and strategic assessments resulting from considerations of international interests constrained the potential military solutions to the internal security problem in Palestine throughout the Arab Rebellion. Because this resulted in a policy that limited the employment of forces and the use of force for units of Jewish character, many potential avenues of utilizing Wingate and his influence with the Jewish community were limited. Wingate, in the end, sacrificed the trust and confidence of his superiors in their perceptions of his utility and loyalty to the Crown and to the British Army in Palestine, when he used methods and channels for voicing his opinions that went beyond those acceptable for an officer of his rank and official capacities. It was his actions in London that brought his political and strategic opinions into question as to whether or not that they could be controlled to remain within the stated policy regardless of what it might be.

Wingate's argument for the British Military to allow, encourage, and stand ready to use an officer with a unique relationship and influence over a portion of the indigenous population while countering rebellion is an interesting one. Wingate's inability to walk the line of appropriateness and professionalism in espousing his opinions, which rightly deserves the criticism that he invites, does not disprove his argument on this point. However, it definitely highlights the difficulty that he also identifies for one playing such a role.

Wingate's rebuttal of the comments in his annual confidential report would eventually be dropped. The reports would not prove to hurt his career, though. This was chiefly due to Sir Archibald Wavell, who Wingate had impressed in Palestine and would become one of his chief military patrons. Wavell recognized Wingate's mind and talent for the "unorthodox." As he would later recall, "I carried away in the corner of my mind an impression of a notable character who might be valuable as a leader of unorthodox enterprise in war, if I should ever have need of one."[184] From Wingate's posting to the Home Guard in the United Kingdom that followed Palestine, he would be summoned by Wavell to work with irregular forces in an unconventional compliment to a conventional campaign in Ethiopia.[185] After successfully aiding in the campaign there, Wavell would shortly thereafter summon him yet again, this time to Burma. There, Wingate would fight, and die, as the commander of the Chindits which he designed and led to operate behind Japanese lines.

Notes

1. The Royal Commission was headed by Lord Peel, and is therefore often referred to in historical works as the "Peel Commission" in order to distinguish it from others; see the official statement of policy from the Colonial Office announcing the Royal Commission, 7 September 1936 in TNA WO 32/4176; J.C. Hurewitz, *The Struggle for Palestine* (New York: Greenwood Press, 1968), 67-68; Christopher Sykes, *Crossroads to Israel: 1917-1948* (Bloomington, IN: Indiana University Press, 1973), 148-149.

2. *Military Lessons of the Arab Rebellion in Palestine, 1936, as published by the War Office, February 1938*, 11-14, 19-20, 36, TNA WO 191/70; Tom Bowden, *The Breakdown of Public Security: The Case of Ireland 1916-1921 and Palestine 1936-1939* (London: Sage Publications, 1977), 222-228; H.J. Simson, *British Rule and Rebellion* (Edinburgh: William Blackwood & Sons Ltd., 1937), 209-210; Yehoshua Porath, *The Palestinian Arab National Movement: From Riots to Rebellion, Volume Two: 1929-1939* (London: Frank Cass and Company Limited, 1977), 197-198.

3. The tactical use of aircraft and their ability to engage rebel bands with machine gun fire and small bombs reached a high level of proficiency in response time and coordination with maneuvering ground forces. Great attention was paid to this capability of close air support, as would be expected with an RAF GOC, but it also appears to have retarded overall intensive efforts by ground forces to innovate and adapt their tactics in order to overcome their repetitive experience of finding themselves at a tactical disadvantage. *Notes on Tactical Lessons of the Palestine Rebellion, 1936*, as published by the War Office, February 1937, 5-7, 15, 19-20; *Military Lessons of the Arab Rebellion in Palestine, 1936*, as published by the War Office, February 1938, 14-15, 159-162, TNA WO 191/70.

4. See the *Notes of Operations in Palestine Between November 1937 and December 1939*, (War Office), 10-11, TNA WO 191/88.

5. *Military Lessons of the Arab Rebellion in Palestine, 1936* (War Office, February 1938), 1-2, 21, 115, TNA WO 191/70.

6. *History of Disturbances in Palestine, 1936-1939* (War Office), Appendix "B", 1-3, TNA WO 191/88.

7. *Military Lessons of the Arab Rebellion in Palestine, 1936* (War Office, February 1938), 17-19, 33, 51, 152-155, TNA WO 191/70.

8. Hurewitz, *The Struggle for Palestine*, 69-70.

9. The TJFF was unique in its flexibility as a "frontier" security force because the Palestinian and Trans-Jordanian border posed no political obstacle to this force. It was run by the Colonial Office under the direction of the High Commissioner in Palestine, and was composed of British officers with soldiers recruited from indigenous populations in both Palestine and Jordan. For a concise summary on their history as well as the British practice of employing such hybrid units in the Middle East, see Matthew Hughes, "British Private Armies in the Middle East? The Arab Legion and the Trans-Jordan Frontier Force, 1920-56, " *RUSI Journal* 153, no. 2 (April 2008): 70-76.

10. *Military Lessons of the Arab Rebellion in Palestine, 1936* (War Office, February 1938), 1, 5-6, TNA WO 191/70. For a description of the command

relationships between the security force commanders and the HC wherein the "civil power kept to itself, not only the right of saying what was to be done, but also the right of saying how it was to be done," see Simson, *British Rule and Rebellion*, 209.

11. Report generated by the Chief Secretary's Office of the Palestine Government, TNA CO 733/313/2; *Military Lessons of the Arab Rebellion in Palestine, 1936* (War Office, February 1938), 118, TNA WO 191/70.

12. Supernumeraries would eventually be categorized into subsets with titles corresponding to either their various functions or their state of permanence within the security forces infrastructure. Examples of these titles include "temporary additional police" and "special constables" among others. For specific debates highlighting the political sensitivities discussed as a result of requests for increases in this force, see the documents contained in TNA CO 733/371/1 and TNA CO 733/359/1; Hurewitz, *The Struggle for Palestine*, 69-70.

13. The Palestine Police were a paramilitary force of mixed British, Arab and Jewish policemen, though predominately Arab. On the whole, the Arabs and Jews were used in communities of their racial affiliation for "traditional" police work (in the modern American sense of the term) with the British element providing the bulk of both supervisory positions and "shock troops." See Bowden, *The Breakdown of Public Security: The Case of Ireland 1916-1921 and Palestine 1936-1939*, 143-176.

14. For a detailed overview of the Palestine Police, their successes and failures, and their falling under military control by September 1938, see the official military document *The Development of the Palestine Police Force Under Military Control*, June 1939, 1, TNA WO 191/90.

15. *Military Lessons of the Arab Rebellion in Palestine, 1936* (War Office, February 1938), 35, 114, 120-122, TNA WO 191/70; Hurewitz, *The Struggle for Palestine*, 69.

16. *Military Lessons of the Arab Rebellion in Palestine, 1936* (War Office, February 1938), 45, 52, TNA WO 191/70.

17. *Military Lessons of the Arab Rebellion in Palestine*, 13, 17, 29, TNA WO 191/70.

18. *Palestine: Information for Commanders of Reinforcing Troops*, 7 September 1936, Part V.2, TNA WO 33/1436.

19. *Military Lessons of the Arab Rebellion in Palestine, 1936* (War Office, February 1938), 13, 21, 30, TNA WO 191/70; "Letter from CIGS to the Secretary of State for the Colonies," 30 June 1936, 4, TNA WO 33/1436.

20. *Military Lessons of the Arab Rebellion in Palestine, 1936* (War Office, February 1938), 13, 21, 30, TNA WO 191/70; "Letter from CIGS to the Secretary of State for the Colonies," 30 June 1936, 4, TNA WO 33/1436.

21. Hurewitz, *The Struggle for Palestine*, 69-71; See "Note of a discussion on the 26th of November 1936 between His Excellency the High Commissioner and General Dill…", TNA WO 32/9401.

22. A series of issuances of Orders in Council and Emergency Regulations

in 1936 and 1937 led to rule by statutory martial law. This was a state of rule between full authority by either the civil power or the military, though one in which the military versus the High Commissioner would eventually maintain the balance of power on issues of security.

23. "Precis of General Dill's dispatch ... dated 30 October 1936," TNA WO 32/9401.

24. See the correspondence between Dill and the CIGS, LHC Dill Collection 2/9.

25. "Precis of General Dill's dispatch ... dated 30 October 1936," TNA WO 32/9401.

26. "Precis of General Dill's dispatch ... dated 30 October 1936," TNA WO 32/9401.

27. "Precis of General Dill's dispatch ... dated 30 October 1936," TNA WO 32/9401.

28. "Memorandum on Point Raised by ... the High Commissioner ... in letter of 15 November 1936," TNA WO 32/9401. For remarks of similar frustrations voiced by the Inspector General of the Police, see Bowden, *The Breakdown of Public Security: The Case of Ireland 1916-1921 and Palestine 1936-1939*, 229-231.

29. *Military Lessons of the Arab Rebellion in Palestine, 1936* (War Office, February 1938), 119-120, TNA WO 191/70.

30. Simson, *British Rule and Rebellion*, 36-53.

31. Simson, *British Rule and Rebellion*, 99-117, 331.

32. Simson, *British Rule and Rebellion*, 4-5, 9-18, 68-69, 77-82, 91-113, 118-128, 200-202, 205-212, 218-219, 220-227, 244, 259, 276-277, 295-297, 306-311.

33. Simson, *British Rule and Rebellion*, 7.

34. For General Dill's deliberations and conclusions on the disposition of units, see the letter from Dill to the CIGS, Field Marshall Deverell, 14 September 1936, LH Dill Collection 2/9, Document 1A.

35. Wingate was an artillery officer, but his fluency in Arabic after having attended language courses and served in the Sudan earned him this intelligence job; Christopher Sykes, *Orde Wingate* (London: Collins, 1959), 102.

36. For insight into Wingate's upbringing as a Christian in the words of his sister and a friend from his days in the Army, see Major General Derek Tulloch, *Wingate: In Peace and War* (London: MacDonald, 1972), 17-20, 44-45; Trevor Royle, *Orde Wingate: A Man of Genius 1903-1944* (London: Frontline Books, 2010), 99.

37. Wingate's Arabic was brought to a high standard after study at the School of Oriental Studies and perfected while serving a five-year tour in the Sudan. See Sykes, *Orde Wingate*, 53-63; Royle, *Orde Wingate: A Man of Genius 1903-1944*, 99.

38. Sykes, *Orde Wingate*, 109-120.

39. The complete text of this letter is very nearly intact between a partial copy of it being preserved in the TBL, File M2313, and its being published in a slightly edited form by Sykes, *Orde Wingate*, 121-125.

40. For commentary on the pro-Arab bias within the military, to include a challenge against the extent to which it has often been claimed, see Simon Anglim, *Orde Wingate and the British Army, 1922-1944* (London: Pickering & Chatto, 2010), 71-73.

41. See Wingate's comments on T. E. Lawrence in his information paper *Palestine in Imperial Strategy*, 6 May 1939, TBL File M2313. Even B.H. Liddell-Hart compares Wingate's actions in Palestine with those of Lawrence. See Liddell-Hart's letter to Winston Churchill (that was accompanied by several of Wingate's documents on the SNS), LHC 15/5/300.

42. Wingate's Jewish contacts included many leading figures that held high positions in the Jewish quasi-government to include those in or with oversight of *Hagana* during the Arab Rebellion. Many would later assume high positions within the Israeli government as well. Antonius was involved primarily as an adviser to Arab Palestinian political figures during the Arab Rebellion. He wrote a highly praised book in 1938 titled *The Arab Awakening: The Story of the Arab National Movement*.

43. Royle, *Orde Wingate: A Man of Genius 1903-1944*, 101-103; Sykes, *Orde Wingate*, 56-57; Derek Tulloch, *Wingate: In Peace and War* (London: MacDonald, 1972), 127-129.

44. Wingate had benefited both from intervention by "Cousin Rex" as well as his own direct approach to meet and influence high-ranking British officers. This helped to shape his career path up to this point. Cousin Rex helped Wingate overcome a deficiency in the qualifications for a position in the Sudan. A direct and personal appeal to the CIGS, General Deverell, resulted in his being selected for a General Staff position (which happened to be Palestine) even though he was not a "qualified" Staff College graduate. See Sykes, *Orde Wingate*, 56-57; Tulloch, *Wingate: In Peace and War*, 43-45.

45. Sykes, *Orde Wingate*, 131-132.

46. The numerous memoirs and books are too many to cite here, but apart from those relationships already noted they include such personalities as General Wavell, General Ironside, Sir Winston Churchill, and Field Marshal Viscount Slim.

47. For Dill's comments on issues of policy as well as his deliberations on military matters from tactical to strategic importance, see LH Dill Collection 2/9, and TNA WO 32/9401;

48. Hurewitz, *The Struggle for Palestine*, 72; For the difficulties faced in "subwar" when a court system is uncooperative with the policy and military strategy, as well the problems posed by the checks and balances inherent in the British system of law that allowed martial and statutory martial law to be challenged, see Simson, *British Rule and Rebellion*, 83-128;

49. For the quotation as cited from Colonial Office documents, see Porath, *The Palestinian Arab National Movement: From Riots to Rebellion, Volume Two: 1929-1939*, 233.

50. Hurewitz, *The Struggle for Palestine*, 73-75.

51. *History of the Disturbances in Palestine 1936-1939: Notes on Operations in Palestine Between November 1937 & December 1939*, 3, TNA WO 191/88; Hurewitz, *The Struggle for Palestine*, 76-82.

52. For the GOC's comments on this period covering rebel activity, military operations, the use of military courts, see his official *Report on the Operations Carried Out by the British Forces in Palestine & Trans-Jordan In Aid of the Civil Power from 12th September 1937 to 31st March 1938*, TNA CO 733/379/3; *History of the Disturbances in Palestine 1936-1939: Notes on Operations in Palestine Between November 1937 & December 1939*, 2-3, TNA WO 191/88; Hurewitz, *The Struggle for Palestine*, 82.

53. *History of the Disturbances in Palestine 1936-1939: Notes on Operations in Palestine Between November 1937 & December 1939*, 3, TNA WO 191/88; Porath, *The Palestinian Arab National Movement: From Riots to Rebellion, Volume Two: 1929-1939*, 233-237, 239; Hurewitz, *The Struggle for Palestine*, 83-84.

54. Porath, *The Palestinian Arab National Movement: From Riots to Rebellion, Volume Two: 1929-1939*, 238-239.

55. Bowden, *The Breakdown of Public Security: The Case of Ireland 1916-1921 and Palestine 1936-1939*, 242-244; Porath, *The Palestinian Arab National Movement: From Riots to Rebellion, Volume Two: 1929-1939*, 239.

56. A sampling of the *Defence Orders in Council* and *Emergency Regulations* can be found in TNA CO 733/39/8; *History of the Disturbances in Palestine 1936-1939: Notes on Operations in Palestine Between November 1937 & December 1939*, Appendix "C", TNA WO 191/88; Bowden, *The Breakdown of Public Security: The Case of Ireland 1916-1921 and Palestine 1936-1939*, 244-245.

57. For a well-researched study on the techniques, legality and cases of excess in the methods used for repressive and punitive military measures, see Matthew Hughes, "A Very British Affair? British Armed Forces and the Repression of the Arab Revolt in Palestine, 1936-1939," *Journal of the Society for Army Historical Research*, (Part One) 87 (351): 234-255, and (Part Two) 87(352): 357-373.

58. For the official reports of this period by the GOC, one in which the rebel bands were reported to have mustered between 300-400 fighters, see *Report on the Operations Carried Out by the British Forces in Palestine & Trans-Jordan In Aid of the Civil Power from 12th September 1937 to 31st March 1938*, TNA CO 733/379/3; *History of the Disturbances in Palestine 1936-1939: Notes on Operations in Palestine Between November 1937 & December 1939*, 2-4, 7, TNA WO 191/88.

59. Tegart was actually chosen to replace the Palestinian Inspector General, but he politely asked to be funded for a trip to assess the situation and then develop recommendations for review by the government before he would entertain such an offer. See his correspondence with the Under-Secretary of State for the Colonies, TNA CO 733/355/8.

60. The British government was eager to implement Tegart's ecommendations, but the speed with which they could do so depended on he height and length of

the bureaucratic path that each was required to travel for approval. See documents addressing Tegart's recommendations and their approval/implementation process in TNA CO 733/383/1.

61. For Tegart's full report on his 28 recommendations submitted for the reform of the Palestine Police, see the documents in TNA CO 733/383/1.

62. *History of the Disturbances in Palestine 1936-1939: Notes on Operations in Palestine Between November 1937 & December 1939*, 4-5, TNA WO 191/88.

63. See the documents located in TNA CO 733/380/13.

64. These settlements were designed as militarily defensible and largely self-sustainable outposts. See Ben-Gurion, "When Bevin Helped Us," *Jewish Observer and Middle East Review,* 4 October 1963; LH 15/5/311; Hurewitz, *The Struggle for Palestine*, 84.

65. For documents on the evolving policy of integration of Jews into the security forces throughout 1938, see TNA WO 32/4176, and TNA CO 733/371/1; For David Ben-Gurion's recounting of the emphasis the Jewish community's leadership placed on seeking positions for Jewish personnel to be integrated into the British security forces, see David Ben-Gurion, "Our Friend: What Wingate Did for Us," *Jewish Observer and Middle East Review*, 27 September 1963, LH 15/5/311; For history of the debate within the Jewish community to press for a standing Jewish security force before the Arab Rebellion, see David Ben-Gurion, "Britain's contribution to Arming the Hagana," *Jewish Observer and Middle East Review*, 20 September 1963, LH 15/5/311.

66. David Ben-Gurion, "Britain's contribution to Arming the *Hagana*," *Jewish Observer and Middle East Review*, 20 September 1963, LH 15/5/311.

67. Tom Bowden, "Policing Palestine 1920-1936," in *Police Forces in History* ed. George Mosse (London: Sage Publications, 1975), 120-121; David Ben-Gurion, "Britain's contribution to Arming the *Hagana*," *Jewish Observer and Middle East Review*, 20 September 1963, LH 15/5/311.

68. See the official Jewish request and the documents on the ensuing British deliberation over a proposal for a Palestinian Frontier Force of thoroughly Jewish character, to include a justification by the requestor by citing the contemporary practice with the Arab Legion and TJFF in TNA CO 733/380/13.

69. For an overview of Wingate's experience in Sudan, see Anglim, *Orde Wingate and the British Army, 1922-1944*, 43-48; Sykes, *Orde Wingate*, 62-63.

70. Sykes, *Crossroads to Israel: 1917-1948*, 124.

71. Sykes, *Crossroads to Israel*, 130-131.

72. Sykes, *Crossroads to Israel*, 131-132.

73. Wingate himself would be requested to establish and lead such units that were either proposed by the Jews or already under consideration by the British in 1942, to include a Jewish "Home Guard," a "Jewish Regiment," and even a special unit of Jewish commandos. See the documents contained in TNA CO 967/96; Jewish requests for such units in 1937 can be found in the documents contained in TNA CO 733/353/11.

74. See documents contained in TNA CO 733/380/13; the one specifically cited here is from General Haining to John Shuckburgh of the Colonial Office, 17 February 1938.

75. See documents contained in TNA CO 733/380/13; the one specifically cited here is from General Haining to John Shuckburgh of the Colonial Office, 17 February 1938.

76. See documents contained in TNA CO 733/380/13, the one specifically cited here is from HC Wauchope to the Colonial Office Secretary of State W.G.A Ormesby-Gore, January 1938.

77. See documents contained in TNA CO 733/380/13, the one specifically cited here is from HC Wauchope to the Colonial Office Secretary of State W.G.A Ormesby-Gore, January 1938.

78. Wauchope's opinion against using Jews for offensive operations on the grounds of its causing irreparable damage to the relationship between the Arab and Jewish communities in Palestine was the origin of this policy. His views can be found in letters to both the military and the Colonial Office as early as 1936. See the documents in TNA WO 32/4178 and TNA WO 32/4176.

79. For the official reports and dispatches on operations by Lieutenant General Haining starting in April and continuing throughout this period, see the documents contained at the LHC, Evetts Collection Box 1-2; *History of the Disturbances in Palestine 1936-1939: Notes on Operations in Palestine Between November 1937 & December 1939*, 3, TNA WO 191/88.

80. See Appendix "A", 1-2 in *History of the Disturbances in Palestine 1936-1939: Notes on Operations in Palestine Between November 1937 & December 1939*, TNA WO 191/88.

81. *History of the Disturbances in Palestine 1936-1939: Notes on Operations in Palestine Between November 1937 & December 1939*, 3, TNA WO 191/88.

82. *History of the Disturbances in Palestine 1936-1939: Notes on Operations in Palestine Between November 1937 & December 1939*, 4, TNA WO 191/88.

83. For the official reports and dispatches on operations by Lieutenant General Haining starting in April and continuing throughout this period, see the documents contained at the LHC, Evetts Collection Box 1-2; *History of the Disturbances in Palestine 1936-1939: Notes on Operations in Palestine Between November 1937 & December 1939*, 5, TNA WO 191/88.

84. In January of 1939, it was recognized that both the military forces conducting internal security duties such as village occupation would eventually have to be replaced, and that the police were still not capable of controlling the security situation. Therefore, it was proposed that the time had arrived to stand up a gendarmerie. The composition of such a force is thoroughly discussed to include the use of Jews, though they rank at the bottom of the list of recommendations that include British, Circassians, Sikhs, Sudanese and Arabs. See *Memorandum Regarding a Gendarmerie or a Semi-Military Force For Palestine* in TNA CO 733/371/6; *History of the Disturbances in Palestine 1936-1939: Notes on Operations in Palestine Between November 1937 & December 1939*, 5, TNA WO 191/88.

85. *History of the Disturbances in Palestine 1936-1939: Notes on Operations in Palestine Between November 1937 & December 1939*, 6, TNA WO 191/88.

86. Based on the Royal Commission's recommendation for partition, a second Royal Commission led by Sir John Woodhead would arrive in April of 1938 in order to investigate the practical application of the partition plan; *History of the Disturbances in Palestine 1936-1939: Notes on Operations in Palestine Between November 1937 & December 1939*, 7, TNA WO 191/88.

87. *History of the Disturbances in Palestine 1936-1939: Notes on Operations in Palestine Between November 1937 & December 1939*, 6-7, TNA WO 191/88.

88. For a description of the military Intelligence section and its officers duties as well descriptions of the other intelligence organizations operating within the government, see *Military Lessons of the Arab Rebellion in Palestine, 1936* (War Office, February 1938), 45, TNA WO 191/70.

89. See Wingate's letter of complaint to his immediate supervisor Wing Comander Ritchie concerning his "confidential report" (evaluation report), 27 June 1939, TBL File M2313.

90. Wingate's immediate supervisor, Ritchie, acknowledged Wingate's fluency in reading, writing, and speaking both Hebrew and Arabic. See Wingate's annual confidential report by Ritchie, 18 November 1938, in TBL M2313; Royle, *Orde Wingate: A Man of Genius 1903-1944*, 111.

91. Wavell would later recount that he "carried away in the corner of my mind an impression of a notable character who might be valuable as a leader of unorthodox enterprise in war, if I should ever have need of one," and he would. See Wavell, *The Good Soldier*, 62; The documents contained in File M2313 at the British Library contain his plan for the reconnaissance as well as an Appendix A: *Narrative attached to Appreciation of arms smuggling*, undated; "Certification for travel for O.C. Wingate," signed by Ritchie, 26 March 1938, TBL M2313.

92. David Ben-Gurion, "Our Friend: What Wingate Did for Us," *Jewish Observer and Middle East Review*, 27 September 1963, LH 15/5/311.

93. "Letter to A.I.P. from Orde Wingate," TBL M2313; For a summary of these events and lessons learned, see also *Appreciation by Captain O.C. Wingate of Force Intelligence on 5.6.38 at Nazareth of the possibilities of night movements by armed forces of the Crown with the object of putting an end to terrorism in Northern Palestine*, IWM, Major General H.E.N. Bredin Files 81/33/1.

94. Hurewitz, *The Struggle for Palestine*, 17-20; Sykes, *Crossroads to Israel: 1917-1948*, 92-94.

95. Sykes, *Crossroads to Israel: 1917-1948*, 162-168.

96. Letter to Wingate from Ritchie, 25 May 1938, TBL M2313.

97. *Force Intelligence Instruction No. 1*, 20 May 1938, TBL M2313.

98. Letter to Wingate from Ritchie, 25 May 1938, TBL M2313.

99. See the official reports on operations during this period in LHC Evetts Collection, specifically, *Haining's Report on the Operations Carried Out By the British Forces in Palestine & Trans-Jordan* both for 1st April to 18th May, 1938, and for 20th May to 31st July, 1938.

100. For the general military assessment of the risks for conducting offensive night operations see *Notes on Tactical Lessons of the Palestine Rebellion, 1936*, as published by the War Office, February 1937, 23-24, IWM Wheeler Collection GB 0099. Wingate had already conducted initial experiments to test some his theories for organization and employment of the force. For the proposal in its entirety, see *Appreciation by Captain O.C. Wingate of Force Intelligence on 5.6.38 at Nazareth of the possibilities of night movements by armed forces of the Crown with the object of putting an end to terrorism in Northern Palestine*, IWM Major General H.E.N. Bredin Files 81/33/1.

101. Wingate's personnel arrived over the first two weeks of June and operations were commenced after a few days of training for each as each squad was formed. Evetts delivered the news in person that the SNS were "officially blessed" on 22 June. See *A Brief History of the SNS Organization, From Its Foundation Towards the End of May, 1938, Until the Departure of Captain O.C. Wingate on 13/10/38* in a letter from Wingate to Evetts, 31 January 1939, TBL M2313, and Lieutenant R. King-Clark's diary at the IWM 83/10/1.

102. Quote by Evetts in Appendix F of *Palestine: Information for Commanders of Reinforcing Troops*, 5, TNA WO 33/1436.

103. These issues are most clearly captured and addressed in *Notes on Tactical Lessons of the Palestine Rebellion, 1936*, LHC GB 0099 Wheeler, and *Military Lessons of the Arab Rebellion in Palestine, 1936*, TNA WO 191/70.

104. *Appreciation by Captain O.C. Wingate of Force Intelligence on 5.6.38 at Nazareth of the possibilities of night movements by armed forces of the Crown with the object of putting an end to terrorism in Northern Palestine*, IWM Major General H.E.N. Bredin Files 81/33/1.

105. *Appreciation by Captain O.C. Wingate of Force Intelligence on 5.6.38 at Nazareth of the possibilities of night movements by armed forces of the Crown with the object of putting an end to terrorism in Northern Palestine*, IWM, Major General H.E.N. Bredin Files 81/33/1, 1.

106. A comprehensive set of Wingate's documents are contained in the LHC 15/5/300, the IWM in the Major General H.E.N. Bredin Files 81/33/1, and at TBL M2313.

107. This analysis is based on the synthesis of the official and personal documents consulted throughout this study. These can be found at the IWM, TBL, LHC and TNA.

108. *Appreciation by Captain O.C. Wingate of Force Intelligence on 5.6.38 at Nazareth of the possibilities of night movements by armed forces of the Crown with the object of putting an end to terrorism in Northern Palestine*, IWM Major General H.E.N. Bredin Files 81/33/1.

109. This analysis is based on the synthesis of documents consulted for this study in relation to the SNS and are contained in the LHC, IWM, TBL, and TNA.

110. *16th Infantry Brigade Operations Instruction No. 20, Night Work*, 4 July 1938, TBL M2313; *Appreciation by Captain O.C. Wingate of Force Intelligence on 5.6.38 at Nazareth of the possibilities of night movements by armed forces of the Crown with the object of putting an end to terrorism in Northern Palestine*,

IWM, Major General H.E.N. Bredin Files 81/33/1.

111. *Appreciation by Captain O.C. Wingate of Force Intelligence on 5.6.38 at Nazareth of the possibilities of night movements by armed forces of the Crown with the object of putting an end to terrorism in Northern Palestine*, IWM, Major General H.E.N. Bredin Files 81/33/1.

112. See Wingate's *Principles Governing the Employment of the Special Night Squads*, 10 June 1938, IWM King-Clark Collection.

113. The influence of Callwell is clearly discernible in Evetts' communications on the necessities for effectively countering rebellion. It is not known whether Wingate was influenced through reading Calwell directly, through Evetts, or through a combination of the two, though Wingate was known for being well read on military matters since a "renaissance" that occurred in his military professionalization during his time at Woolwich. For the reference to Wingate's military professional "renaissance," see Sykes, *Crossroads to Israel: 1917-1948*, 38-42; for an analysis of Callwell's influence on Evetts' and Wingate's thoughts, see Anglim, *Orde Wingate and the British Army, 1922-1944*, 76-80.

114. See Evetts remarks in Appendix F of *Information for Commanders of Reinforcing Troops*, TNA WO 33/1436.

115. Wingate would later attribute to Evetts that it was his "enthusiasm and understanding alone [that] made my experiment [the SNS] possible." See Wingate's *Palestine in Imperial Strategy*, 6 May 1939, TBL File M2313.

116. *16th Infantry Brigade Operations Instruction No. 20, Night Work*, 4 July 1938, TBL M2313.

117. *Appreciation by Captain O.C. Wingate of Force Intelligence on 5.6.38 at Nazareth of the possibilities of night movements by armed forces of the Crown with the object of putting an end to terrorism in Northern Palestine*, IWM Major General H.E.N. Bredin Files 81/33/1.

118. These types of operations are numerously recounted in the reports on operations throughout this period of the rebellion. See the reports and dispatches on operations found at the LHC Evetts Collection Box 1-2.

119. *A Brief History of the SNS Organization, From Its Foundation Towards the End of May, 1938, Until the Departure of Captain O.C. Wingate on 13/10/38* in a letter from Wingate to Evetts, 31 January 1939, TBL M2313.

120. Several of Wingate's official reports on SNS operations can be found between TBL File M2313 and LHC 15/5/300. King-Clarke's narrative of several operations can be found in IWM King-Clarke collection 83/10/1. An overview of the SNS actions as recorded by Wingate can be referenced in *A Brief History of the SNS Organization, From Its Foundation Towards the End of May, 1938, Until the Departure of Captain O.C. Wingate on 13/10/38* in a letter from Wingate to Evetts, 31 January 1939, TBL M2313.

121. See Wingate's official report, *Report of Operation Carried Out By Special Night Squads on the Night of 11th/12th July 1938, By Captain O.C. Wingate, O.C.S.N.S*, 22 July 1938, LHC 15/5/300.

122. See *A Brief History of the SNS Organization, From its Foundation*

Towards the End of May, 1938, Until the Departure of Captain O.C. Wingate on 13/10/38 in a letter from Wingate to Evetts, 31 January 1939, TBL M2313.

123. See Wingate's "*Palestine in Imperial Strategy,*" 6 May 1939, TBL File M2313.

124. See Wingate's official report *Action of Special Night Squads on Night 3rd/4th September, 1938*, 4 September 1938, LHC 15/5/300.

125. See the official dispatch in TNA CO 733/379/3.

126. See Wingate's official report *Action of Special Night Squads on Night 3rd/4 th September, 1938*, 4 September 1938, LHC 15/5/300.

127. See *A Brief History of the SNS Organization, From its Foundation Towards the End of May, 1938, Until the Departure of Captain O.C. Wingate on 13/10/38* in a letter from Wingate to Evetts, 31 January 1939, TBL M2313.

128. See *A Brief History of the SNS Organization, From its Foundation Towards the End of May, 1938, Until the Departure of Captain O.C. Wingate on 13/10/38* in a letter from Wingate to Evetts, 31 January 1939, TBL M2313.

129. See *A Brief History of the SNS Organization, From Its Foundation Towards the End of May, 1938, Until the Departure of Captain O.C. Wingate on 13/10/38* in a letter from Wingate to Evetts, 31 January 1939, TBL M2313.

130. The Liddell Hart Center contains the most complete set of these documents on the SNS that were written by Wingate to include his proposals, principles governing their employment, notes on the their development, reports on their operations, standing orders, and a document on their organization and training. See LHC 15/5/300. Some of these documents are also found at the Imperial War Museum, and they are referenced in this paper. Note that some of the documents by the same title have been re-typed as copies on different sizes of paper, therefore the page numbers are not always congruent between the reports held by different institutions.

131. "Appreciation by Captain O.C. Wingate of Force Intelligence on 5.6.38 at Nazareth of the possibilities of night movements by armed forces of the Crown with the object of putting an end to terrorism in Northern Palestine," 6, IWM, Major General H.E.N. Bredin Files 81/33/1.

132. See *Principles Governing the Employment of the Special Night Squads*, 1, June 1938; *Note on the Development of Special Night Squads...*, 1-2, 14 July 1938, LHC 15/5/300;

133. Letter from BG Evetts to Force Headquarters, September, 1938, TBL File M2313.

134. See Haining's *Report on the Operations Carried Out By the British Forces in Palestine & Trans-Jordan, Period 20th May to 31st July, 1938*, 6, LHC Evetts Collection Box 1-2.

135. See Haining's *Report on the Operations Carried Out By the British Forces in Palestine & Trans-Jordan, Period 20th May to 31st July*, 1938, 7, LHC Evetts Collection Box 1-2.

136 . *Appreciation by Captain O.C. Wingate of Force Intelligence on 5.6.38 at Nazareth of the possibilities of night movements by armed forces of the Crown*

with the object of putting an end to terrorism in Northern Palestine, 1, IWM Major General H.E.N. Bredin Files 81/33/1.

137. For a British military officer to be specifically mentioned in an official dispatch was an honor that was even recorded among official military awards and decorations as a notable event in an officer's career.

138. For Wingate's initial intentions to operate along the pipeline then expand operations elsewhere, see *Principles Governing the Employment of Special Night Squads*, 1, LHC 15/5/300.

139. See Wingate's letter to Evetts in which he recounts the purpose and history of the SNS (verifiable by Evetts), 31 January 1939, TBL M2313.

140. *Principles Governing the Employment of the Special Night Squads*, 1, June 1938, LHC 15/5/300; "Note on the Development of Special Night Squads ...", 1, 14 July 1938, LHC 15/5/300.

141. *A Brief History of the SNS Organization, From Its Foundation Towards the End of May, 1938, Until the Departure of Captain O.C. Wingate on 13/10/38* in a letter from Wingate to Evetts, 31 January 1939, TBL M2313.

142. This was a result of the employment of security details that were at various times and in various combinations conducted by units of largely Jewish character either by the IPC company or infrastructure security units acting in combination with police and military forces.

143. David Ben-Gurion, "Our Friend: What Wingate Did for Us," *Jewish Observer and Middle East Review*, 27 September 1963, LH 15/5/311; See *Principles Governing the Employment of the Special Night Squads*, 1, June 1938, LHC 15/5/300.

144. See the letter from the HC to the Secretary of State for the Colonies, 2 July 1938, in TNA WO 32/4176.

145. Letter from Secretary of State for the Colonies Malcolm MacDonald to HC Harold MacMichael, 22 August 1938, TNA CO 733/371/1; The HC's report, when compared to the GOC's report, captures some interesting nuances concerning their timing and style in breaching the topic that they had agreed as "better to ask for forgiveness than for permission," though it cannot be determined how much of this is a result from organizational culture versus personal style.

146. For this debate in detail as it circulated between the primary military and political advisers and decision makers, see the documents contained in TNA WO 32/4176 and TNA CO 733/371/1. There are references in this debate concerning the authority of this policy that point back its establishment in an interdepartmental meeting that took place in January of 1937.

147. See the documents in TNA WO 32/4176, specifically the letter from the HC to the Secretary of State for the Colonies; for the admission by commander of HM Forces in the ME that "I had made up my mind to arm the Jews and to withdraw most of the troops" if war broke out in the fall of 1938; see the letter from General Ironside to Wingate, 8 June [1939], TBL M2313.

148. See the reference to this request in the "Telegram from the High Commissioner for Palestine to the Secretary of State for the Colonies," 11 September 1938, TNA WO 32/4176.

149. *Telegram from the High Commissioner for Palestine to the Secretary of State for the Colonies*, 11 September 1938, TNA WO 32/4176.

150. *The Development of the Palestine Police Force Under Military Control*, June 1939, 1, TNA WO 191/90.

151. Sykes. *Crossroads to Israel: 1917-1948*, 175-176; Wingate would openly state his expectation for the SNS trained Jewish supernumeraries to become noncommissioned officers and potentially officers if and when the expected war between the European powers escalated. For one such example, see Wingate's letter to Wing Commander Ritchie contending his confidential report (officer evaluation report), 27 June 1939, TBL File M2313.

152. For the official military reports on this entire period, see the two following reports. *Report on the Operations Carried Out by The British Forces in Palestine & Trans-Jordan: Period 1 August to 31 October, 1938*, 30 November 1938, TNA CO 733/379/3; *Dispatch on Operations Carried Out by the British Forces in Palestine & Trans-Jordan: Period 1 November, 1938 to 31 March, 1939*, 24 April 1939, LHC Evetts Collection Box 1-2.

153. "History of the Disturbances in Palestine 1936-1939: Notes on Operations in Palestine Between November 1937 & December 1939," 8-9, TNA WO 191/88; Hurewitz, *The Struggle for Palestine*, 94.

154. For an overview of Arab and Muslim countries with regard to their cooperation in international politics as well as their evolving relationships with Axis powers, see Martin Kramer, *Islam Assembled: The Advent of the Muslim Congresses* (New York: Colombia University Press, 1986), 167-171; Bernard Lewis, *From Babel to Dragomans: Interpreting the Middle East* (New York: Oxford University Press), 167-171; for the anxiety and impact of these issue within the British government, see Sykes. *Crossroads to Israel: 1917-1948*, 190.

155. Porath, *The Palestinian Arab National Movement: From Riots to Rebellion, Volume Two: 1929-1939*, 277-281.

156. See the official report by the Criminal Investigation Division in Palestine on the Jewish Revisionist political organization and the *Irgun Tvai Leumi* militant organization, as well as the effects of their being targeted, August 1938, TNA CO 733/386/8.

157. See the letter from Haining to Directorate of Military Operations and Intelligence, 19 January 1939, LHC O'Connor Box 3/4.

158. Hurewitz, *The Struggle for Palestine*, 93.

159. Hurewitz, *The Struggle for Palestine*, 93.

160. Hurewitz, *The Struggle for Palestine*, 93.

161. See Wingate's letter to his mother, 2 August 1938, TBL File M2313.

162. See Wingate's complaint to Ritchie on his annual confidential report, 27 June 1939, TBL File M2313.

163. Sykes, *Orde Wingate*, 185, 193-194.

164. The most extensive work on Wingate's activities during this leave period is recorded by Sykes, who conducted many interviews for otherwise

unattainable information, although he does not cite all of his material in detail. See Sykes, *Orde Wingate*, 188-194.

165. For later documents written by Wingate in addition to those already cited in this work, see *Palestine in Imperial Strategy*, 6 May 1936, and *Plan for Employment of Jewish Forces in the Prosecution of War*, 13 October 1939, TBL File M2313.

166. David Ben-Gurion, "Table Talk with Lord Lloyd," *Jewish Observer and Middle East Review*, 13 December 1963, LH 15/5/311;

167. See the letter to Lord Lloyd from CIGS Gort, 1 November 1938, TBL File M2313.

168. See the letter from Liddell Hart to Churchill, 11 November 1938, LHC 15/5/300; For the Churchill-Wingate meeting at a dinner party, see Sykes, *Orde Wingate*, 192-193.

169. Sykes, *Orde Wingate*, 190.

170. Sykes, *Orde Wingate*, 194.

171. *A Brief History of the SNS Organization, From its Foundation Towards the End of May, 1938, Until the Departure of Captain O.C. Wingate on 13/10/38* in a letter from Wingate to Evetts, 31 January 1939, TBL M2313.

172. See Wingate's complaint to Ritchie on his annual confidential report, 27 June 1939, TBL File M2313.

173. For Haining's official military reports on this period, see *Report on the Operations Carried Out by The British Forces in Palestine & Trans-Jordan: Period 1 August to 31 October, 1938*, 30 November 1938, TNA CO 733/379/3. O'Connor, one of Haining's division commanders, also summarized the strategy of this period with special attention to his area of operations in the south. See O'Connor's *Operations in Palestine 1938–1939*, LHC O'Connor Files Box 1.

174. *Report on the Operations Carried Out by The British Forces in Palestine & Trans-Jordan: Period 1 August to 31 October, 1938*, 30 November 1938, 8, TNA CO 733/379/3.

175. Hurewitz, *The Struggle for Palestine*, 94-113; Porath, *The Palestinian Arab National Movement: From Riots to Rebellion, Volume Two: 1929-1939*, 256-260, 281-294.

176. See Wingate's appointment orders, 11 May 1939, TBL File M2313.

177. See Wingate's annual confidential reports by Ritchie, 18 November 1938 and 9 June 1939, and by Haining, 10 July 1939, in TBL File M2313.

178. See Wingate's annual confidential report by Haining, 10 July 1939, in TBL File M2313.

179. See Wingate's complaint to Ritchie on his annual confidential report, 27 June 1939, TBL File M2313.

180. Sykes, *Orde Wingate*, 194.

181. Sykes, *Orde Wingate*, 144.

182. See Wingate's complaint to Ritchie on his annual confidential report,

27 June 1939, TBL File M2313.

183. *Military Lessons of the Arab Rebellion in Palestine, 1936*, as published by the War Office, February 1938, 28-37, TNA WO 191/70.

184. See Wavell's personal recollection of Wingate as recorded in a written account at the IWM 97/20/10, Wingate Chindit Papers, Box 5.

185. Orde Wingate led irregular forces in Ethiopia in 1940 and 1941 to Great Britain's first "victory" of World War Two. Archibald Wavell, Commander in Chief of all British Forces in the Middle East, had summoned him. The British strategy resulted in the provision of conventional and unconventional military support to restore Haile Selassie to his throne after the Italian invasion resulted in his being expelled.

Chapter 5
Conclusion

Orde Wingate sought to shape the evolving British internal security strategy at the tactical, operational, and strategic levels. Tactically, he developed and employed a system of organization and associated tactics to be employed as both a counterguerrilla specialist unit and as a test bed for capturing and disseminating tactical and training "lessons learned." Operationally, he proposed a plan to expand his organization and tactical methods for counterguerrilla operations to be conducted on a widespread and sustainable basis in order to bring rural areas under governmental control. Strategically, he envisioned the formation of security forces of Jewish character as capable of securing British interests in Palestine as well as furthering British strategic interests in the Near East.

Wingate's attempts to shape the overall military strategy can be considered to take place by means of two primary avenues. The first was through a bottom-up proposal to reform organizational and tactical methods in order to solve a tactical and operational military dilemma. The second was through influencing the policy makers for top-down reform of policy governing the composition and employment of the internal and external security apparatus in Palestine. Wingate used many methods to achieve these effects, to include proofs of concept, writing information papers, disseminating his ideas through military reports, personal contacts and correspondence, and meeting with policy makers or those who were influential among them.

Tactically, Wingate was able to employ successful tactical and organizational innovations within the unit that he secured to operate under his command, the SNS. He was enabled by his ability to analyze and synthesize the applicable lessons learned of his own experience and that of others. These included those of his military commanders, the official Lessons Learned of the campaign in which he was participating, and most probably the small wars' traditions (though this latter connection cannot be supported through concrete evidence). Wingate excelled (1) in his understanding and abilities for analysis of the operational environment; (2) the use of intelligence in targeting; (3) maximizing the psychological element of operations to achieve desired effects; (4) organization of tactical units to maximize effectiveness; and (5) employing effective techniques for tactical engagement of guerrillas.

Despite the tactical successes of this force and its methods, there were three primary factors that mitigated Wingate's success in achieving his intentions to impact the internal security strategy at the operational and strategic levels. His intentions were to reshape the composition and employment of security forces towards expanded use of Jewish personnel without restrictions on the types of operations that they could undertake.

The mitigations and their causes were:

1. The failure of widespread adoption of his tactics due to a surge in British Military Forces which rendered the tactical risks inherent in his methods to be deemed unacceptable;

2. The prevention of operational expansion due to the composition of his organization in friction with a policy that restricted the strength and employment of Jews within the security forces; and

3. The loss of trust from the military command toward Wingate due to his crossing the accepted boundary of a military official's obligation to submit his own opinions to established policy.

The study of Wingate and his actions in Palestine have potential for modern relevance in numerous military domains. A study of Wingate's confrontation with the tactical and operational dilemmas of the Arab Rebellion reveal the process and skills necessary for a practitioner to identify military problems and formulate solutions. The details that are revealed have utility for general military use, and they will be especially beneficial in their specifics to units concerned with counterguerrilla and counterterrorist operations.

Furthermore, some topics are proposed for further study and consideration as a result of this case study.

First, the military mechanisms and roles of officers in:

1. Tactical, operational and strategic reform during a campaign; and

2. Advising policy-makers on policy.

Wingate did not initially occupy a position within the military hierarchy that included responsibilities and authorities for the reform of tactics. He was never in this type of position with regard to formulation of strategy. He was therefore outside the chain of responsibility and authority for making recommendations and decisions on these issues until he interjected himself into the process. No military officer is ever truly outside the domain of concern with regard to these issues, and every military organization inherently has mechanisms that officers of various rank and position can leverage to influence the campaign. These mechanisms can be official or unofficial, robust or scarce in opportunity, and accepted or unaccepted as either stated by rules or implicit by general consensus. The outlets for an officer to address concerns outside of his area of responsibilities and authorities can be destructive, neutral, or constructive to the military organization. Whether expressed concerns take the shape of complaints, comments or recommendations, the channels through which they are communicated and the audiences to whom they are expressed are key in determining which of the three effects will be achieved.

Officers and officials within the British security forces in Palestine chose many different routes to communicate their opinions, ideas and criticisms. A few notable examples: (a) Simson wrote a book; (b) the Inspector General of the Palestine Police wrote a letter to the editor of a newspaper; (c) officers captured Lessons Learned of the campaign on a wide variety of topics for widespread distribution (and in a timely enough manner to influence the campaign); and (d) the GOC and Chief of the Imperial General Staff communicated officially and unofficially to occupants of higher, parallel, and lower-level positions in both the military and political realms on a variety of issues of concern, both within and outside of their official capacities for duties.

Wingate, as a junior military officer, wrote "appreciations" and memorandums blending critical analysis of current issues outside of his scope of responsibility and authority with proposed solutions for consumption by senior leaders. Militarily, these issues included those of strategic argument, operational employment, tactical reformation, and organizational composition. Beyond his written communications, he secured personal meetings with senior military officers through personal requests and introductions by patrons.

Military culture usually embodies a logical framework for the general determination of what is appropriate and inappropriate for such communications. Policies restricting particular forms or methods concerning the actions of military members in doing so are often enacted to clarify the rules of staying within one's "lane." These rules are often emplaced in reaction to challenges of the military culture's guidelines. These issues of appropriateness for the methods and content of officers voicing their concerns when outside of the responsibility and authority hierarchies require further consideration. Such consideration should especially address both the organizational utility of such concerns when expressed in a constructive manner, as well as the mechanisms that might be available to promote this utility. The course of this research has shown history to highlight the importance of junior officers in campaigns of countering rebellion. Modern COIN commanders might consider the importance of these officers not only for what they contribute tactically to the fight, but how their analysis of the operational environment might contribute to the body of knowledge upon which tactical, operational and strategic decisions are made.

Second, the potential roles and utilization of junior officers with unique abilities, experiences, and influence within a military organization and campaign.

Another issue that this study highlights that is worthy of addressing in future works is the capacity of a military organization to identify and utilize junior leaders with unique abilities, experiences, and influence. Efforts can be made to place them in positions that best use these assets for furthering a military organization's goals. Wingate's experience in Palestine (and especially his ensuing experiences in Ethiopia and Burma) show that elements of the British Army during this period were capable of flexibility in assignments, award of rank, and organizational flexibility.

In Palestine, Wingate was selected to serve as an intelligence officer despite his official function as an artillery officer. This was based on his language abilities and having served long-term in the Arab world. He was then heard out and supported in his proposal of a proof-of-concept and given command of an ad hoc unit. It is also worth noting that Wingate's influence among the Jewish leadership was both recognized and factored in to minor decisions in Palestine. The recorded experiences of this occurring, however, were a result Wingate's direct requests rather than an intentional plan that was initially formed or later expanded to exploit his influence's potential.

After Palestine, he would be hand-selected to participate in the British Campaign in Ethiopia where he was involved with the British emplacement of Haile Selassie as political and military ruler in opposition to the Italian-backed regime. During World War II, Wingate would be promoted well beyond the standard paradigm associated with time in grade in order to organize and command the Chindits. The beneficial aspects of these types of flexibility should be explored and compared to the modern strictures of the officer career path, as well as with the award of rank and its associated positions. Furthermore, the concept of talent management and the use of officers with unique experiences, abilities, and influence should be explored for greater utilization of the utility that they offer the military as an organization.

Third, a historically based formulation of modern doctrine for conducting warfare of small-wars legacies is best utilized in its application by historically informed practitioners within the officer corps.

In consideration of the Small Wars tradition from which Wingate hailed, the methodological approach of Small Wars literature deserves further examination. Even if the military practitioners accept that the doctrine has gotten it "right," however, this still only consists of half of the equation as the particularities of the situation at hand will always require the use of judgment in its application. An officer's individual operational experiences, education, and access to synthesized and disseminated "lessons learned" as a campaign progresses all inform this judgment. While each of these is a valuable contributor, there is yet another contributor that not only acts in this same capacity but also serves a further purpose. Breadth and depth of historical knowledge concerning the peculiarities of warfare relevant to the campaign that a practitioner is waging acts both as a mental compass and to give perspective when personal experience and education fail to adequately inform. History informs doctrine, and history must also inform the practitioner in its application.

For commanders, staffs, campaign planners, and junior officers, their judgment is shaped by these same guides as they participate in their portion of the process to analyze the operational environment, define the problem sets, develop a military strategy, identify operational goals and approaches, develop effective tactics, employ their force(s), and make adjustments on all of the above as the situation develops. An effective staff and trusted inner circle will no doubt be a weapon that an astute commander will employ in creating a similar environment to that of the doctrine writer so that his observations, assumptions, and visualization of the battlefield takes the shape of a sound, coherent, and communicable approach that has undergone the rigors of intellectual examination and cross examination. A more historically informed officer corps should produce a significantly better appreciation of the environments in which they are expected to perform, as well as a more sound application of doctrine in their roles, as both commanders and commanders' confidants.

A significant contribution of Small Wars literature appears to be found in the approach that it took toward preparing and equipping the officer corps to best use the aspects of their tradition, experiences, and best practices that were earned over a long history. The means was a combination of emphasis and style for communicating its history. This history was communicated in depth and detail in conjunction with pithy maxims and summarized concepts. The inclusion of numerous historical references provided the basis for detailed examination, explanations and conclusions that were intended to guide and inform the proper judgment of the one referencing it, according to his particular circumstances, for application. The traditional approach to Small Wars literature was written by practitioners for practitioners, with the purpose of providing military officers a few broad principles and many examples to guide their conduct in Small Wars. The historical background from which these principles were drawn was not neglected, but rather it was recognized as an integral part of the process from which others could and should learn. Callwell acknowledges the universality of ideas such as principles of war that were derived from studying war in general, but he goes on to note that "the conditions of small wars are so diversified, the enemy's mode of fighting is often so peculiar, and the theatres of operations present such singular features, that irregular warfare must generally be carried out on a method totally different," and that the "conduct of small wars is in fact in certain respects an art by itself. ... " He adds that "the strategical problems presented by operations of this nature have not altered to [a great] extent. Therefore there is much belonging to this branch of the military art still to be learnt from campaigns dating as far back as the conquest of Algeria and as the terrible Indian struggle of 1857-58. ... " He concludes that principles "can be learnt from the military history of early times just as well as it can be learnt from the more voluminously chronicled struggles of the present epoch."[1]

Militaries should consider an organized and progressive program, designed to equip their officer corps to employ a historically informed approach to their application of doctrine commensurate with their expected levels of responsibility and command. The process of inculcating this historical knowledge base should be started early. Officers should be sufficiently grounded in the history of the potential forms of warfare in which they are expected to participate, and they should be engaged throughout the military education phases of their career with opportunities to continue building and exercising the "historical" element of their professional education and abilities. The realm of "self-development" should not be relied upon to serve this function, but should complement an organized, focused, and resourced approach to equip the officer corps with a strong historical character in its pursuit of building and maintaining a professional force.

Professional military education venues should be used to support an organized evolution of the officer's knowledge and understanding of relevant history as well as the skills needed to handle and employ it. This process could include:

1. A survey of military history in order to create "width" of historical knowledge;

2. Rigorous analysis of case studies from the tactical to strategic levels relevant by virtue of the types of operations conducted and their regional focus in order to create "depth" of historical knowledge; and

3. An emphasis on the use of original sources for the process of research, analysis, synthesis, and formulating and defending a thesis in order to build and hone the abilities to interact with, critically evaluate, and communicate historical knowledge.

These objectives should increase the officers' capacity to both know and then properly "use" relevant history, such as employing the necessary skills required for critical evaluation of the transferability of historical "lessons" from one context to another.

An insightful and concise framework for educating military officers in the art of war by means of a historically based approach has been proposed by Professor Michael Howard in his article "The Use and Abuse of Military History." He states:

> Three general rules of study must therefore be borne in mind by the officer who studies military history as a guide to his profession and who wishes to avoid pitfalls. First, he must study in width. He must observe the way in which warfare has developed over a long historical period. Only by seeing what does change can one deduce what does not; and as much as can be learnt from the great discontinuities of military history as from the apparent similarities of the techniques employed by the

great captains through the ages. ... Next he must study in depth. He should take a single campaign and explore it thoroughly, not simply from official histories, but from memoirs, letters, diaries ... until the tidy outlines dissolve and he catches a glimpse of the confusion and horror of real experience ... and, lastly, he must study in context. Campaigns and battles are not like games of chess or football matches, conducted in total detachment from their environment according to strictly defined rules. Wars are not tactical exercises writ large. They are ... conflicts of societies, and they can be fully understood only if one understands the nature of the society fighting them. The roots of victory and defeat often have to be sought far from the battlefield, in political, social, and economic factors which explain why armies are constituted as they are, and why their leaders conduct them in the way they do. ... It must not be forgotten that the true use of history, military or civil ... is not to make men clever for the next time; it is to make them wise forever.[2]

A systematic approach to guiding and developing a more historically informed officer corps would not be a wasted effort in the money, time, and rigor invested. It would produce a generation of officers acting as commanders, staff, peers, and subordinates that is more competent in how they think about and execute their missions, as guided by appropriate historical contexts. It would enable them to more effectively employ their force and its capabilities in war—and all this regardless of whether they had the "right" individual experiences to best prepare them, or even whether the doctrine had gotten it "right" or "wrong." According to Clausewitz, "Historical examples clarify everything. ... This is particularly true of the art of war."[3]

Fourth, considerations for establishing Wingate's influence on Israeli military thought and practice.

Wingate's attempts to change British policy for using Jews within the security forces on a large scale, to include forming a Jewish Army, were not successful. While Wingate's tactical methods and operational plans held the greatest potential for impact on the British internal security strategy, a different lens must be used to evaluate his potential impact on Israeli Military thought and practice. Though this subject goes beyond the supported evidence offered in the research and thesis presented here, some points are offered that could prove useful for readers interested in how Wingate's actions in Palestine might relate to later Israeli development of military thought and practice.

Numerous points of comparison could be drawn between Israeli Military thought and practice and Wingate's emphases. For illustration, just two points are mentioned here: the psychological effects of tactical dominance, and the preeminence of particular Principles of War (i.e., surprise).[4] While such lines of influence would most certainly be difficult to prove, two points are worth noting. First, many prominent Israeli Military soldiers and leaders shared the experience of having Wingate as their first "professional" military commander. While this influence might appear on the surface to be minor, the significance of the impact should not be underestimated. Many a soldier can recount even their most early experiences of serving under such an able and respected leader as Wingate. Such experiences can deeply shape a soldier's military mind. The fact that Wingate would be requested by name to return to Palestine to stand up a Jewish security force during World War II reveals the extent of this impact. This point is particularly poignant given that it took place before Wingate had undertaken the Chindit operations in World War II, for which he is best known in the Western world. Second, many memoirs and interviews by Israeli Military professionals would later reveal their personal accounts of his powerful influences upon them.

Notes

1. C.E. Callwell, *Small Wars: Their Principles and Practice* (London: Harrison and Sons, 1906), 23.

2. Michael Howard, "The Use and Abuse of Military History." *RUSI Journal* (February 1993; reprint from 1961), 29-30.

3. Carl von Clausewitz, *On War* (edited and translated by Michael Howard and Peter Paret. Princeton, NJ: Princeton University Press, 1984), 170.

4. A copy of Wingate's training notes for the SNS is a part of the IWM Wingate collection 2/1. "Surprise" is listed as number one among the principles of war.

Bibliography

Primary Sources

The National Archives (TNA), Kew, UK
Cabinet (CAB): 106/648.
Colonial Office (CO): 732/81/9-10, 733/39/8, 733/313/2, 733/350/22, 733/353/11, 733/355/8, 733/359/1, 733/371/1-2, 733/371/6, 733/372/8, 733/372/10, 733/379/3, 733/380/13, 733/383/1, 733/386/8, 733/386/13, 733/386/23, 733/387/1, 733/410/11, 967/96.
Security Service (KV): 5/33.
War Office (WO): 32/4176, 32/4562, 32/9401, 32/9497, 33/1436, 191/65, 191/67, 191/70, 191/73, 191/88, 191/90, 201/169, 201/2134, 206/2018A, 216/46, 216/111.
The Imperial War Museum (IWM), UK
Orde C. Wingate Collection: 2/1.
H.E.N. Bredin Collection: 81/33/1.
Rex King-Clarke Collection: 83/10/1.
The British Library (TBL).
Microfiche Film Collection, M2313.
Liddell Hart Center (LHC) for Military Archives, King's College, London
Dill (Field Marshall Sir John Greer) Collection, Box 2.
Evetts (Lieutenant General Sir John) Collection, Boxes 1-2.
Liddell Hart (Captain B.H.) Collection, 11/1938/37, 11/1938/149, 15/3/71-72, 15/5/297-299, 15/5/300, 15/5/311.
O'Connor (General Sir Richard) Collection, Boxes 1-3.
Wheeler (Major General Thomas Norman Samuel) Collection.

Government Documents

The Division of Near Eastern Affairs for the U.S. Department of State, The Mandate for Palestine, dated 1927, reprinted as The Palestine Mandate (Documentary Publications; Salisbury, NC, 1977).
General Staff Army Headquarters, Delhi, India, Operations in Waziristan 1919-1920, dated 1923, reprinted by The Imperial War Museum Department of Printed Books, The Naval and Military Press Ltd, East Sussex, 2011.
War Office. Duties in Aid of the Civil Power, 1937.
War Office. Notes on Imperial Policing, 1934.
War Office, N.W. Frontier of India 1936-1937, Official History of Operations, reprinted by The Imperial War Musuem Department of Printed Books, The Naval and Military Press Ltd, East Sussex, 2010.
War Office. *Training Regulations*. London: War Office, 1934.

Secondary Sources

Anglim, Simon. *Orde Wingate and the British Army, 1922-1944*. London: Pickering & Chatto, 2010.
Anglim, Simon. Strategic and Combat Studies Institute Occasional Paper Number 49–Orde Wingate, The Iron Wall and Counterterrorism in Palestine, 1936-1939 (Swindon: Director of Defence Studies, 2004).
Antonius, George. *The Arab Awakening*. Safety Harbor: Simon Publications, 2001.

Asprey, Robert. *War in the Shadows: Volume One.* New York: Doubleday, 1975.
Beckett, Ian. *Modern Insurgencies and Counter-Insurgencies: Guerrillas and their Opponents since 1750.* London: Routledge, 2001.
Beckett, Ian, ed. *The Roots of Counter-Insurgency: Armies and Guerrilla Warfare, 1900-1945.* London: Blandford Press, 1988.
Begin, Menachim. *The Revolt: Story of the Irgun.* Jerusalem: Steimatzky, 1977.
Ben-Eliezer, Uri. *The Making of Israeli Militarism.* Bloomington, IN: Indiana University Press, 1998.
Bierman, John, and Colin Smith. *Fire in the Night: Wingate of Burma, Ethiopia and Zion.* New York: Random House, 1999.
Bowden, Tom. *The Breakdown of Public Security: The Case of Ireland 1916-1921 and Palestine 1936-1939.* London: Sage Publications, 1977.
Bowden, Tom. "Policing Palestine 1920-1936." In *Police Forces in History,* ed. George Mosse, 120-121. London: Sage Publications, 1975.
Callwell, C. E. *Small Wars: Their Principles and Practice.* London: Harrison and Sons, 1906.
Charters, David, and Maurice Tugwell. *Armies in Low-Intensity Conflict: A Comparative Analysis.* London: Brassey's Defence Publishers, 1989.
Churchill, Winston. *Step By Step: 1936-1939.* London: Thornton Butterworth Ltd, 1940.
Clausewitz, Carl von. *On War.* Edited and translated by Michael Howard and Peter Paret. Princeton, NJ: Princeton University Press, 1984.
Duncan, Andrew, and Michel Opatowski. *War in the Holy Land: From Megiddo to the West Bank.* London: Sutton Publishing, 1998.
Fergusson, Bernard. *The Trumpet in the Hall 1930-1958.* London: Collins, 1970.
French, David. *Raising Churchill's Army.* Oxford: Oxford University Press, 2000.
Fromkin, David. *A Peace to End All Peace.* New York: Henry Holt and Company, 1989.
Haythornthwaite, Philip J. *The Colonial Wars Source Book.* London: Arms and Armour, 2007.
Heilbrunn, Otto. *Warfare in the Enemy's Rear.* New York: Praeger, 1963.
Hurewitz, J. C. *The Struggle for Palestine.* New York: Greenwood Press, 1968.
Gwynn, Sir Charles. *Imperial Policing.* London: Macmillan and Co., 1935.
Gwynn, Charles. *Imperial Policing.* London: Macmillan and Co., 1939. Internet edition, 2004, http://www.combatreform.org/PENTOMICARMYAGAIN/imperialpolicing.htm.
Kedourie, Elie. *Politics in the Middle East.* Oxford: Oxford University Press, 1992.
Keegan, John, ed. *Churchill's Generals.* New York: Grove Weidenfeld, 1991.
Kitson, Frank. *Bunch of Five.* London: Faber and Faber, 1977.
Kramer, Martin. *Islam Assembled: The Advent of the Muslim Congresses.* New York: Colombia University Press, 1986.
Lewis, Bernard. *From Babel to Dragomans: Interpreting the Middle East.* New York: Oxford University Press.
Mead, Peter. *Orde Wingate and Historians.* Braunton: Merlin Books, 1987.
Mockaitus, Thomas. *British counter-insurgency in the post-imperial era.* Manchester: Manchester University Press, 1995.
Mosley, Leonard. *Gideon Goes to War.* New York: Charles Scribner's Sons, 1955.

Porath, Yehoshua. *The Palestinian Arab National Movement: From Riots to Rebellion, Volume Two: 1929-1939.* London: Frank Cass and Company Limited, 1977.

Rid, Thomas and Thomas Keaney. Understanding Counterinsurgency: Doctrine, operations, and challenges. London/New York: Routledge, 2010.

Royle, Trevor. *Orde Wingate: A Man of Genius 1903-1944.* London: Frontline Books, 2010.

Sachar, Howard M. *A History of Israel: From the Rise of Zionism to Our Time.* 2nd ed. New York: Alfred A. Knopf, 2003.

Segev, Tom. *One Palestine, Complete: Jews and Arabs under the British Mandate.* London: Albacus, 2000.

Simson, H. J. *British Rule, and Rebellion.* Edinburgh: William Blackwood & Sons Ltd., 1937.

Strachan, Hew. *Big Wars and Small Wars: The British army and the lessons of war in the twentieth century.* London: Routledge, 2006.

Sykes, Christopher. *Orde Wingate.* London: Collins, 1959.

Sykes, Christopher. *Crossroads to Israel: 1917-1948.* Bloomington, IN: Indiana University Press, 1973.

Thesiger, Wilfred. *The Life of My Choice.* New York: W.W. Norton & Company, 1987.

Townshend, Charles. *Britain's Civil Wars: Counterinsurgency in the Twentieth Century.* London: Faber and Faber, 1986).

Tulloch, Derek. *Wingate in Peace and War: An Account of the Chindit Commander.* London: MacDonald, 1972).

Van Crevald, Martin. *The Sword and the Olive: A Critical History of the Israeli Defense Force.* New York: Public Affairs, 2002.

Wavell, Archibald. *Good Soldier.* London: MacMillan, 1948.

Periodicals and Articles

Anglim, Simon. "Orde Wingate and the Special Night Squads – A Feasible Policy for Counter-Terrorism?" *Contemporary Security Policy,* 28, No. 1 (April 2007): 28-41.

Cohen, Michael. "Secret Diplomacy and Rebellion in Palestine, 1936-39." *International Journal of Middle East Studies* 8, No. 3 (July 1977): 379-404.

Denning, B. C. "Modern Problems of Guerrilla Warfare." *Army Quarterly and Defence Journal* 13 (1927): 349.

Howard, Michael. "The Use and Abuse of Military History." *RUSI Journal* (February 1993; reprint from 1961).

Hughes, Matthew. "A Very British Affair? British Armed Forces and the Repression of the Arab Revolt in Palestine, 1936-1939." *Journal of the Society for Army Historical Research*, (Part One) 87 (351): 234-255.

Hughes, Matthew. "A Very British Affair? British Armed Forces and the Repression of the Arab Revolt in Palestine, 1936-1939." *Journal of the Society for Army Historical Research*, (Part Two) 87 (352): 357-373.

Hughes, Matthew. "British Private Armies in the Middle East? The Arab Legion and the Trans-Jordan Frontier Force, 1920-56." *RUSI Journal* 153, No. 2: (April 2008): 70-76.

Hughes, Matthew. "The Banality of Brutality: British Armed Forces and the

Repression of the Arab Revolt in Palestine, 1936-1939." *English Historical Review* 124:507 (March 2009): 313-54.

Mackey, Robert M. "Policing the Empire." *Military History* 24, No. 5 (July/August 2007): 26-35.

Strachan, Hew. "The British Way in Warfare." *Oxford History of the British Army* (Oxford: Oxford University Press, 1994): 403-408.

Townshend, Charles, "The Defence of Palestine: Insurrection and Public Security, 1936-1939." *The English Historical Review* 103, No. 409 (October 1988): 917-949.

Other Sources

Alderson, Alex. "The Validity of British Army Counterinsurgency Doctrine after the War in Iraq 2003-2009." Ph.D. dissertation, Cranfield University, 2009.

Mockaitis, Thomas. "The British experience in counterinsurgency, 1919-1960." Ph.D. dissertation, The University of Wisconsin, Madison, 1988. Published by UMI, Ann Arbor, 1989.

www.ingramcontent.com/pod-product-compliance
Lightning Source LLC
Chambersburg PA
CBHW050503110426
42742CB00018B/3352